Fears to Fierce

A WOMAN'S GUIDE TO OWNING HER POWER

BRITA FERNANDEZ SCHMIDT

Executive Director of Women for Women International

RIDER

1

Rider, an imprint of Ebury Publishing,
20 Vauxhall Bridge Road,
London SW1V 2SA

Rider is part of the Penguin Random House group of companies
whose addresses can be found at global.penguinrandomhouse.com

Penguin
Random House
UK

First published by Rider in 2021

www.penguin.co.uk

A CIP catalogue record for this book is available from the British Library

ISBN 9781846046513

Printed and bound in Great Britain by Clays Ltd, Elcograf S.p.A.

The authorised representative in the EEA is Penguin Random House
Ireland, Morrison Chambers, 32 Nassau Street, Dublin D02 YH68.

Penguin Random House is committed to a sustainable future for our
business, our readers and our planet. This book is made from Forest
Stewardship Council® certified paper.

MIX
Paper from
responsible sources
FSC® C018179

To Emma and Sara.
May you follow your fierce.

Contents

Foreword

We are all called at some point in our lives to answer some basic questions. How should we live? What are we here for? What is our purpose? What makes a meaningful life. Not all of us are brave enough to answer that call. But, those of us who do decide to make that journey of discovery need companions and a guide.

We first came across Brita through her incredible work for the charity Women for Women International. At the time we had just finished writing our own guide for women seeking purpose – *WE: A Manifesto for Women Everywhere* – and were researching charities that supported women for the resources section of our book. We quickly found ourselves in awe of Women for Women International's transformative work with women in conflict zones around the world. And, equally inspired by Brita, it's fearless, fierce leader, who had an inner light and energy that it is impossible not to be captivated and motivated by.

We have witnessed Brita's courage and leadership, her ability to light up a room and win support for some of the most vulnerable women on the planet. Three years on it is an honour and a privilege to write the foreword to her guide which we're sure will touch the lives of many women.

Brita generously lays out her own journey, the role of feminism and the vital importance for humanity of inspiration. She weaves her experiences and wisdom in and out of the equally inspiring stories of women she has met along the way. She shares the actions and techniques that have helped her connect with her truth, her passion and her purpose.

Fears to Fierce is a wonderful, inspiring book for women seeking to find their purpose. She coins the term 'Fierce' to describe that light within us that burns more brightly the more inspired we are and the more connected we are to our inner truth. It is not for the fearful, but as Brita writes, and we both know from our own inner work, 'everything you need is already within you'.

We wish you luck as you embark on finding your 'fierce' – the force that will lead you to live fully and help to transform the world.

Gillian Anderson and Jennifer Nadel, authors of *We: A Manifesto for Women Everywhere*

Introduction

'Life's a journey not a destination.'

– Lynn H. Hough[1]

I f I could choose a superpower, it would be the power to inspire. When I'm inspired, I feel I can move mountains, overcome fears and follow my dreams. I feel a surge of energy that speaks to the very essence of who I am. I call this my fierce. When something inspires me, it is my fierce that responds. I call it my 'fierce' because when I follow it, I allow my true power to shine without holding back. 'Fierce' also implies feral wildness, something that is not tainted or touched by the norms that are learned and govern our everyday lives.

I want you to feel like that, too.

Sometimes, our surroundings can lead us to lose touch with our fierce and be overcome by fear. As we are taught societal norms and expectations from an early age, we also learn to fear what will happen if we don't abide by these conventions. And feeling fear stops us being true to our fierce, because our fierce most probably doesn't make us feel 'normal'. We instinctively know that nurturing our fierce will mean departing from the norm. And that means putting ourselves on the outside, where we fear we will be alone and not accepted or loved.

[1] Lynn H. Hough, *The Christian Advocate* (The Sunday School Lesson: First Quarter, Lesson IX, 1920)

Here's the thing – I believe the majority of us feel like this. I am yet to meet someone who feels 'normal'. We all have our own fierce and we are all scared to be fully true to it, because it will mean being 'different'. But if we allow ourselves to stop and realise that most of us feel like this, we begin to create the foundations for positive change in our own lives, and beyond. Embracing what our fierce is telling us will help us to redefine our own lives, and in turn it will affect those around us.

One of the most important parts of this redefinition is a move away from labelling everything either/or. We imprison ourselves by defining our lives within the constraints of binaries such as light and dark, good and bad, right and wrong, with or against. We urgently need to create an alternative discourse that allows us to talk about our uncertainties, our hopes, our doubts, our thought processes, our realities, our messiness and be okay with that. We need to find a way to be okay with ourselves as we are right now, without fear, embracing our fierce.

Even writing this, it is so hard not to include a value judgement: fear is 'bad' and fierce is 'good'. But looking at it in this way doesn't help us. At the heart of the fears to fierce journey is an awareness and understanding of ourselves, not labelling. If we are to free ourselves and determine what truly works for us and our fierce, questioning those labels and moving beyond them to understand who we are, what we really think and feel and what our fierce is telling us, is so important. That self-leadership is at the core of *Fears to Fierce*.

Moving towards a place where we channel our own values is particularly hard because the boxes we are put into right from when we are children are firmly focused on controlling our power so as not to disrupt the status quo. For as long as I can remember, I knew I was expected to be a 'good girl', to please, and to fear not being liked. All the while, the power within us wants to emerge. My personal journey of striving to be true to my passions and connect to the fire in my belly has shown me that the answer – a meaningful and purposeful life – was within me all along. The change we are seeking, the impact we want to create, begins with looking within.

In *Fears to Fierce*, I invite you to listen to your inner power because *you* are the change. As we commit to ourselves and stop questioning our fierce, the doubt and fear that we have been brought up with dissolve, and we accept our own power. Our impact on the world around us shifts. We start to see how our own transformation inspires change in others and we realise we are not alone.

This book will guide you towards this transformation by walking you through three key stages: Find meaning; Own your power; Transform your world.

Find meaning

When we allow ourselves to connect to how people or experiences make us feel, we open ourselves up to feeling inspired. When we're inspired, our fierce fires up. This is where we'll discover what matters to us; the purpose of our life. Defining what is meaningful to us – why we are here, what we want to do and who we want to be – helps us realise that it is up to us to follow that path. To do so, we need to tap into our power in ways that we have not done before, which leads me to ...

Own your power

Many of us feel that we are discouraged from feeling powerful. I remember as a teenager being told to be quiet by my father. I had a distinct feeling that I was *too much*. I felt that I had to quieten my fierce in order to fit in. Becoming acquainted with and embracing our power can be petrifying, but cultivating self-leadership is at the heart of the fears to fierce journey. I will share with you the story of how I stepped into my power, and offer practical actions that you can take to do the same.

My experience has shown me that there are four key anchors that help us to lead ourselves and be 'in' our power and this section is structured around them: trust, strength, love and care.

Transform your world

As we embrace our power, our transformation will become visible to ourselves and to others, and we will see our impact. At first, acknowledging and becoming comfortable with the impact we'll have is as difficult as owning our power. But through this section, you'll come to learn that we create an impact just by being who we are. With practice, we can become attuned to how we make people feel. The more we become aware, the more deliberate we can be about our intentions, and the greater our impact will be. Nurturing deep empathy with others and learning how to act on it allows us to make changes where we choose: in our families, at work, or in our communities. Our impact in turn will inspire others to embrace their power and create a sense of shared humanity, and so the ripples of impact go on. In this way, we realise that we are all activists.

The transformation that this book will guide you through requires commitment and determination. This is not a quick fix or a silver bullet, but a way of fundamentally shifting how we live our lives and how we feel about ourselves and others. The change will sometimes be difficult – painful, even – but *Fears to Fierce* will be your guide. I want you to know that you are not alone. I know how hard change is and it does not happen overnight, so I have designed this journey to provide help and support.

At the end of each chapter, you'll find a summary of the key lessons you'll have learned, plus an 'Action' section to help you practise these lessons in your own life. Many of the actions will ask you to reflect, to tune in to your body, to listen deeply to yourself. This transformation is holistic, and occurs when we tap into all of our body, mind, heart – and our fierce. Before you begin, I suggest buying yourself a special notebook and pen to use as you read the book – you can jot down thoughts, feelings and observations and use it to complete some of the suggested actions at the end of each chapter.

As you embark on your fears to fierce journey, start with a commitment to **be kind to yourself no matter what**. Sometimes just reading a chapter and letting it sink in is all you'll need to do. You get to decide what works for you.

As I offer you *Fears to Fierce*, I want you to know that in the attempt to bring clarity to the chaos that is life, there is the inevitable risk that it sounds fabricated, too good to be true, a little too neat. I have tried my best to add as many challenges and as much messiness to the book as I can. I want you to know that, even though I've travelled the fears to fierce journey many times, I don't have all the answers. Most days I have a moment where I feel fearful and don't trust myself. Don't forget that. I am real, like you, and real means messy.

But here is a really important message:

Everything you need is already within you.

What this book is about – at its heart – is *rediscovering* your fierce ... fully, truly, gloriously. It's a process whereby you come home – to yourself. Along the way, you'll inspire those who are witnessing your transformation to do the same. In this way, your self-leadership is in fact the biggest impact you can ever have.

So, as you venture forth on your fears to fierce journey, know that you are the hero of your story. You are the change you are dreaming of.

PART I

Find Meaning

Chapter 1

Inspiration

Ignite your fierce

'Dance as though no one is watching,
Love as though you have never been hurt before,
Sing as though no one can hear you,
Live as though heaven is on earth.'

— William W. Purkey

My fierce

I remember landing in Venezuela, aged 15. When I left the air-conditioned airport building, the inescapable equatorial heat enveloped every part of my body, in a way that made me feel that nothing would ever be the same. This was a world far from the small town where I'd grown up, Borgholzhausen, in Germany. Large families chattered, excited to have their loved ones back, taxis with their windows open blasted the beats of merengue music, palm trees moved in the soft evening breeze.

As my parents, younger brother and I were driven from the airport in Maiquetia to Caracas, our driver decided to show us the scenic route instead of taking the fast motorway, so we could see more of the city that was going to be our new home.

It was already dark as we drove through the city's shanty towns, past houses that did not look to me like houses. Many did not have windows, just holes; a few were makeshift, erected from little more than cardboard boxes. I remember wondering what would happen when the rainy season came. That thought worried me, made me sad. I didn't understand why people had to live like this, but I knew it wasn't right.

Before arriving in Venezuela, I had never been to a country with real poverty. There were a lot of people out on the streets, talking, standing around. The driver told us to lock the car doors and close our windows. To this day I don't know why he decided to show us the shanty towns on that first evening, but he did – and what he said scared me. Just as the heat had hit me when I left the air-conditioning of the airport, so did the poverty I saw that night as we drove into Caracas. It hit me in my stomach, into my core. That night a spark ignited deep in my being – my fierce had woken up.

As we settled into life in the city, it was not just the poverty that shook me, but the obvious and stark inequality. Alongside the shanty towns, there were mansions with swimming pools, country clubs, wealth like I had never seen before. I couldn't understand it. My brother and I went to the Colegio Humboldt, where my father had got a job as a teacher. Apart from the other teachers' children, most of the pupils were from German expat families much wealthier than we were. I learned very quickly that there were clear unspoken hierarchies of worth. People with big SUVs, swimming pools and servants believed they were more important than anyone else. It became clear that teachers were worth less.

Until then, I'd never thought about the fact that my parents were teachers. I knew my mother really loved being a teacher and her pupils would give her great gifts at Christmas and stay in touch long after she'd stopped teaching them. I thought what she did was brilliant. It was only after arriving in Venezuela that I became aware there are people who look down on teachers and, by extension, their children.

In Venezuela, teachers were perceived as providing a paid-for service. And in this new world where I was now living, those whose service you paid for were not treated as equals. As if just because you pay for something it gives you the right to treat someone without respect. I was angry and disgusted when I realised how this mindset infiltrated people's thinking. Money and the status associated with it became the centre of the universe. You started to evaluate yourself based on what you had, in which part of town you lived. Without even realising, you started to see yourself through the eyes of that mindset. I dealt with it by pretending I didn't know it was happening. I pretended the people I was interacting with did have respect for my parents and did not discriminate against me because I was the daughter of their teacher. It was never spoken about, but I saw it in their eyes, their demeanour. I did not have the language for it, but I saw how this inequality affected everyone, creating a divide between them and us. You were either wealthy and you wanted to surround yourselves with other people of the same social status, or you were not and it was expected that you should aspire to being so.

But I didn't want to aspire. It was not right that people were living in makeshift houses while others were in huge mansions; it was not right that people were valued according to their job titles or their belongings. I felt overwhelmed. There were days when I felt heat rising within me and I wanted to cry and scream at the injustice. I knew that I had to do something. I wanted to go out and tell everyone that it didn't matter what your name or your profession was, or who your parents were: we were all worth the same as each other.

I saw class-based and economic inequality, which seeped through Caracas like a stream, and, in time, I became aware of gender inequality too. Gladys was a woman who worked for my parents, helping us in the house. She came every day in the morning at 8am and left in the evening at 4pm. She was a young single mother with four children all under the age of ten, and all by different men. She told me that each of those men had left her. We would chat every day, often after school in the kitchen while she was preparing *buñuelos*, a typical maize dish that I loved. She had dreams and hopes, above all for her children and her youngest daughter in particular. I had an urge to tell her that she didn't have to let herself be treated like this by men. I felt angry for what had happened to her. Why were the fathers of her children so irresponsible? And why would she allow them to treat her like this? But at the same time, I admired her strength. She worked hard: on weekends she had another job cleaning offices. She wanted to make sure that her children could go to school. Despite the challenges and hardship of being a single mother and the heartache of losing men she'd loved, she did not give up. Gladys was the first woman whose fierce inspired me.

Meanwhile, I began to see that gender inequality was also playing out in my own family. One night at the dining table, after we'd finished eating, my father asked me to help my mum clear the table, while he and my brother, Alex, just sat there. I didn't know anything about feminism at the time, but I definitely knew that this was not right. There it was again, that same feeling. Why did I have to help tidy and yet my brother didn't? 'And what about Alex?' I said. I don't remember my dad saying anything.

Venezuela had awoken my fierce. I couldn't understand it and I found my feelings overpowering. There would be days where I would take the bus with my best friend Manuela, the only other person I knew who was experiencing similar feelings, to sit at the foot of Mount Avila, the most beautiful mountain in Caracas. We would talk about how misunderstood we felt, about how wrong society was, and our dreams of a different world. My fierce was a powerful force, but I didn't know what to do with it.

The inequality between women and men had slapped me in the face. It was suddenly apparent in my daily life. I learned there were rigid expectations and rules of behaviour for girls that you had to abide by in order to be liked and accepted.

I could see that girls who were softly spoken, who displayed feminine, subservient qualities – rolling their eyes, twiddling their hair and smiling coyly – were more loved. I found it hard to behave like that because it made me feel uncomfortable and dishonest. I felt so torn, because I did want to be accepted and loved, but I didn't want to be false. It meant that I was labelled as different – and that never feels good, especially for a teen. I was different because I was difficult, loud and too much. 'Brita, can you just calm down'; 'Brita, please can you just be quiet'; 'Brita, just let it go'.

But I didn't want to let it go.

Being labelled different, difficult, loud, too much made me feel sad and inappropriate. I concluded there was something fundamentally wrong with me. My character and my body were not right. I lost my confidence. I tried hard to turn into someone else, someone who would fit in. I was constantly trying to lose weight so that I would be more petite. I would wear clothes that were feminine and I tried to be a really good girl, helping in the house, doing my homework, following the rules, looking up to adults and showing respect even when I didn't feel like it. I wanted to be accepted and loved, and I decided that for that to happen, my fierce had to be tamed.

The power of inspiration

It was only when I arrived at the University of Essex five years later and took a course called Feminist Literary Criticism that I remember feeling, for the first time, that maybe I did not have to be someone else. Perhaps the problem was bigger than me. That course, and my subsequent MA in Women's Studies at the University of Sussex, gave me access to the language I needed to speak about what I was feeling. And it was a language that many women before me had spoken and were still speaking.

I was not alone.

I met other women who had had similar experiences to mine. Learning about their lives and struggles inspired me. It made me feel I could follow my fierce and do something about this deep fire within me. There was Jeong-won from South Korea and Nadimeh from Syria. Together we read books by great women writers from all over the world: Toni Morrison, Jeanette Winterson, Nawal El Saadawi, Luisa Valenzuela, Clarice Lispector, Virginia Woolf, Alice Walker and many more. The three of us became good friends. We could not have been more different, but when we sat together and spoke about the position of women within our respective societies, we saw ourselves reflected in each other. This was inspiration in action.

I was in a perpetual state of being inspired by the bravery and strength of women, and in turn I felt strong myself. I read about amazing women from across the world and across the centuries. The fierce women who survived the Chinese Communist Revolution, the brave women who lived during the nineteenth-century Industrial Revolution in Great Britain, German women who survived the Holocaust, Argentinean women who defied the dictatorship in the 1970s. Wherever I looked there were examples of women breaking the rules, defying the norms. Understanding how women before me had followed their fierce and their dreams despite the obstacles that society had put in their way inspired me.

What I experienced at university became life-changing and would set my path in a direction that meant I would always seek to surround myself with women who inspired me with their fierce. I experienced then what I know now: **as I witness another woman's rising, she gives me wings.**

How does inspiration appear?

Inspiration helped me to reconnect with my fierce when I was at university, and has been a guiding force in my life ever since.

Allowing yourself to be inspired is the greatest gift you can give yourself. Think of inspiration as the fuel for your fierce.

To be inspired is allowing yourself to feel what you want to do and believing you can do it! It's easier said than done, but I know we all have the ability to tune in to what inspires us and use it as a tool to overcome fears and follow our fierce because I've been doing it for years.

Inspiration comes when you see a reflection of yourself in someone or something, or see someone or something as a reflection of you. You are inspired when you allow yourself to connect deeply to what it says or conveys.

Nature inspires me. I go running every morning – always the same route – and about halfway through there is a beautiful tree next to a small stream. Every morning I stop there and take three deep breaths in front of that tree. My daughter Sara calls it the giving tree, probably because of the peace it gives to me. Seeing the tree change over the seasons and yet be there always rooted deep in the earth is magical. It inspires me because of its strength and permanence. That is what I want to see reflected in me.

But, most of all, it is people who inspire me. For the past 25 years I have worked with women all over the world: in the UK, Germany and the US, but also in more than 15 countries where the organisations I have worked for operate, including Ethiopia, Iraq, Nigeria, Rwanda, Bosnia and Kosovo. I've had the honour of gaining an insight into their lives, their traumas, their hopes, their dreams, their realities. I have seen the important role that inspiration has played for them, in exactly the same way that it has for me, because every woman I have met has told me about someone who has inspired her. I know it is this – more than anything else – that gives us all the strength to overcome challenges and follow our dreams.

Nothing has a greater power to help me overcome my fears than the inspiration I feel when I read or hear about other women who follow their fierce. I get goosebumps from their stories of defiance in the face of fear and I am moved by their power to transform their lives. They inspire me to be true to myself because their stories show me that I am not alone. I can trace my life and the decisions I have made by the people who have inspired me.

In 2005, I read *Between Two Worlds: Escape from Tyranny – Growing Up in the Shadow of Saddam* by Zainab Salbi, the founder of Women for Women International. Zainab's father was Saddam Hussein's pilot, and she gives an insight into how stifling, oppressive and scary it was to grow up in Iraq, and in such close proximity to Saddam Hussein himself. At the end of the book, Zainab tells the story of how, in 1993, she set up Women for Women International in the US.

The way she described her reasons for establishing it and the impact it had moved me deeply. Her message of sisterhood and creating connections with women in countries affected by conflict reverberated within me in the most profound way. I really wanted to work for the organisation but it was based in Washington DC, with no office in the UK.

Fast-forward two and a half years. I had been working for another women's rights organisation in the UK, Womankind Worldwide, for ten years, and I was ready for a different challenge. One afternoon, I was contacted by headhunters for Women for Women International, who had been tasked with finding a director to grow the organisation in the UK. I could not believe what I was hearing. Three years after being deeply inspired by Zainab's book, I met her and she offered me my dream job. Of course, I said yes – and here I am, a decade on, executive director at the organisation whose mission had moved me so deeply all those years ago.

Inspiration is everywhere. In 2016, I was asked to give a keynote speech at a women's leadership conference. As I sat down to write it, I realised that there was far more I wanted to say than I could fit into 45 minutes. Sitting at my kitchen table, I distinctly remember feeling that this could be the beginning of a book. That was nearly four years ago – and here we are.

Inspiration is also infectious. It spreads like wildfire, if you allow it. When we allow ourselves to be inspired, we inspire others. Iliriana Gashi is the director of the Women for Women International programme in Kosovo and she told me that Zoja, one of the trainers on the life skills programme that the organisation runs, inspires her every day. Zoja gives women skills, confidence and access to new knowledge, but also pure, unconditional love. I know Zoja and it shines right out of her.

Zoja told me that Remzije, a woman she trained, inspires her. Remzije lost her husband in the Kosovan war and was left alone and destitute. When she enrolled in the programme with Zoja, Remzije fully embraced the opportunity and believed that she could transform her life. Remzije showed her exceptional dedication and as a result she is now employed by Women for Women International in Kosovo, earning an income and providing for her children. Remzije has told me about another woman who had inspired her – and so the chain of inspiration continues.

Inspiration as transformation

If we allowed ourselves to be inspired, we would live in a different world. Much of the inequality we see is rooted in our inability to be inspired by each other, to connect with each other, and to see our own reflections in each other.

We are so preoccupied with fulfilling our own aspirations that we forget that we don't exist in silos. My dreams are your dreams. We are linked in our aspirations as human beings. History shows us that when we forget about our interconnectedness it comes back to haunt us. I believe that if we turn a blind eye to human rights abuses, starvation, injustice and poverty, because they don't directly affect our personal well-being right now, we are failing our own humanity.

How can you be ambitious for yourself and not also for the rest of humanity? That is what sits at the heart of inequality. Whenever we elevate ourselves at the cost of others, we fail humanity.

Allowing ourselves to be deeply inspired is our opportunity to tap into our shared humanity. I know that inspiration is good for me and it is good for you and it is good for us together.

In short, it is a win-win-win!

So, how do we regain our ability to be inspired?

A few years ago, when the Syrian crisis was intensifying and ISIS captured thousands of Yezidi girls, I could not stop thinking about them. In August 2015, one year after the girls were captured, I was on holiday with my family. We were in France, and had rented a holiday home with a beautiful garden for our new puppy, Bruno. Our daughters Sara and Emma were 12 and 15 and we spent the weeks going for bike rides, swimming and playing games. I felt full of happiness and gratitude.

Then, one morning after breakfast, I read an article in the *New York Times* about a 12-year-old Yezidi girl, who had been held as a sex slave for 11 months and repeatedly raped during that time. It described how the Islamic State fighter bound and gagged her, then kneeled beside the bed and prostrated himself in prayer before getting on top of her. When it was over, he kneeled to pray again, bookending the rape with acts of what he would have considered religious devotion.[2]

The girl had managed to escape, making her – somehow – one of the lucky ones. Even so, every time I thought of her, I cried. I kept thinking that this could have been Sara, my own 12-year-old daughter, who was so full of life, so excited about her blog, so happy and carefree.

The young Yezidi girl could have been my daughter.

I had to do something to help Yezidi women. When I got back from holiday, I spoke to my team at Women for Women

[2] www.nytimes.com/2015/08/14/world/middleeast/isis-enshrines-a-theology-of-rape

International. We were in the middle of organising a fundraising dinner and decided that we would ask guests to make donations to help Yezidi women so that Women for Women International could start a programme in the Kurdistan region of Iraq. This would help Yezidi women and girls rebuild their lives after the traumatic experiences suffered at the hands of ISIS.

I thought a lot about the speech I was going to give at the gala. So much rested on it. How could I inspire guests to feel what I had felt when I read the article? How could I share this passion that I was feeling and the urgency I felt to help?

I started my speech by telling the audience about Emma and Sara, and the joyful summer holiday we'd just returned from. Then I told them about my third daughter, the 12-year-old girl who had just escaped from the Islamic State where she had been held captive and repeatedly raped. 'She is traumatised and I cannot bear to think about what has happened to her,' I said. 'She is not physically my daughter, but she could have been.'

That evening, we raised £850,000, an unprecedented amount of money, and have since been able to use some of it to help over 1,400 Yezidi women in partnership with a local organisation, the Free Yezidi Foundation.[3] Women for Women International supported the creation of a safe space in Khanke camp, a refugee camp for Yezidis in Dohuk, northern Iraq. Yezidi women and girls received psychosocial counselling as well as information about their rights, and they were taught skills, including learning English, using a computer and handicrafts.

This is just one story, but it demonstrates that **when we allow ourselves to be inspired, to connect and see ourselves reflected in each other, everything changes.** Our fear dissipates, inaction is no longer an option, and we know we will find a way. The power of inspiration is infinite. I know that the more I allow myself to be inspired, the more I can inspire others – it's a chain reaction. That night my fierce was fuelled because I was inspired by the 12-year-old girl who'd survived. It allowed

[3] www.freeyezidi.org

me to connect with the guests in the room in a way that moved them profoundly and inspired them to do what they could. In this way, we can all connect with global events on an individual level and leverage our power to help – something we'll come on to later in the fears to fierce journey.

Feel the fear and do it anyway

The process of seeking inspiration, allowing it to flood your body and mind, and then acting on it, isn't easy, but most, if not all, things in life require hard work and commitment. Allowing yourself to be inspired is no different. If only we were taught at school how to hold on to the invincibility we feel as children. It seems that somewhere between the ages of ten and 15, we stop acting on inspiration. We develop fears – and fears keep us from acting on inspiration.

We still feel the inspiration, but a split second later we tell ourselves, 'Don't be silly, you could never do that!' We find a million reasons why we should forget about the spark of inspiration we felt and become engulfed in fear: the fear of not being accepted, the fear of not being enough, the fear of not fitting in.

The solution? We need to relearn how to act on inspiration.

I read Susan Jeffers's[4] book, *Feel the Fear and Do It Anyway*, when I was 38. A wonderful woman and friend, Sarah Clark, gave me the book for my birthday, the day before I started my new role at Women for Women International. You know those serendipitous moments, when you are given the right book at the right time? That was it for me. This book not only helped me with starting a new job but significantly influenced my life. In it, Jeffers explains how to face fear, and why we should:

In all my life I have never heard a mother call out to her child as he or she goes off to school, 'Take a lot of risks

[4] Susan Jeffers, *Feel the Fear and Do It Anyway* (Hutchinson, 1987)

today, darling.' She is more likely to convey to her child, 'Be careful, darling.' This 'Be careful' carries with it a double message: 'The world is really dangerous out there' ... and ... 'You won't be able to handle it.' What Mom is really saying, of course, is, 'If something happens to you, I won't be able to handle it.

I want to feel the fear and do it anyway. Even aged 15, as we were driving towards Caracas, I knew instinctively that I did not want the fear I felt to be my catalyst for change.

My daughters, Emma and Sara, inspire me every day to drive myself forward and allow myself to be fierce and, in turn, I want to inspire them to know they are enough. That they can be who they want to be: they can roar and be loud and big or small and quiet – it is up to them. I commit to turning my fears to fierce every day so that I can say to Emma and Sara: 'Take risks. Know you are enough. Be inspired.'

And I am saying this to you, too.

The key to transformation is to feel inspired and then to act on this inspiration. There are actions you can take now to begin straight away: commit to feeling inspired; learn what inspires you and why, and share this feeling with others; create a new habit and practise doing this. The steps in this chapter's action plan will help you get started ...

Lessons learned

We all have the capacity to be inspired.

We can all inspire.

We fuel our fierce by inspiration.

We will all be fulfilled and happier if we allow ourselves to be inspired.

Being inspired allows us to connect as human beings.

Inspiration is the catalyst for transformation.

Inspiration is key for humanity.

Actions

The tasks below will help you connect to your inspiration so that you may begin the process of transformation:

1. **Goosebumps**
   Think about the last time you got goosebumps and write it down. Do this regularly, and you will start to see patterns about what inspires you.

2. **Actively feel inspiration**

- Think about something that has inspired you.

- Tell one other person about it – really take time to describe how the person or what you heard made you feel and what you would love to do now as a result. What did it ignite in you? Have you felt this before? Just telling another person will solidify the inspiration within you. Saying what happened out loud is an important step towards acting on that spark. Don't worry about what it might sound like, or that it sounds strange in your head – just do it. There are more tips on how to ignore that niggling negative voice in chapter 4.

- Once you have told another person about what inspired you, stop for a moment and reflect on what happened. How did you feel? In addition, reflect on the reaction of the person who you were sharing your inspiration with. If you can, note it down. At the beginning you might find this hard, but be patient and tune in to your feelings. How did your inspiration manifest in the person you told?

3. **Your fierce needs food!**

- **Social media:** Deliberately curate your Instagram and other social media feeds – set aside time to follow people who inspire you and look at their feeds regularly. Unfollow anyone who makes you feel the opposite.

- **Podcasts:** I listen to podcasts most mornings on my run. The *SuperSoul Sunday* recordings with Oprah Winfrey never fail me! For other podcasts that lift me up see my suggestions at the end of the book.

- **Notebook:** When you read something or hear something that inspires you, write it in your notebook. Then, when you are in need of inspiration, take the book and randomly open it. Read what you wrote on that page. It will always be exactly what you need to hear in that moment.

- **Boardroom in your heart:** This is my favourite action and I think you're going to love it. I have created a boardroom in my heart where the most important humans who have inspired me deeply and have changed my life sit round the table.

I can go to my boardroom whenever I need to and they'll be there for me, to remind me of my resolve. They cheer me on. They inspire me. I invite you to start creating your own boardroom in your heart right now. Who will get the first chair? And as you continue going through the chapters, you can add more humans.

For now, focus on these actions. In the next chapter, we'll begin to turn your inspiration into a purpose.

Chapter 2

Purpose

Express your fierce

'And so we need to hope for the realization of our own dreams, but also recognize a world that will remain wilder than our imaginations.'

– Rebecca Solnit, *Hope in the Dark*[5]

More often than not, we define ourselves by the jobs we have. They are the public definition of our worth. What is your job? What position do you hold in your company? What salary are you on? What is your career plan?

Before I had defined my purpose, I didn't like it when people asked me these questions. At the time, I didn't know exactly why I didn't like it. I think it was partly because I didn't have a career plan, so I felt I was failing, and partly because I felt they were really pointless questions. My job title is not the most important piece of information I want people to have about me.

If I am asked now, I talk about my purpose. I say that no matter where I work or live or what job title I might have, I will always focus on my purpose.

I think about my purpose as an articulation of my fierce. Fulfilling my purpose might include wanting to become a

[5] Rebecca Solnit, *Hope in the Dark* (Canongate, 2016)

director, because I believe it can accelerate my ability to achieve my purpose, but I am clear that being a director is not the aim. It is the means to fulfilling my purpose.

Shift your thinking towards purpose, not career! It's revolutionary. For example, take childcare as performed by stay-at-home parents: there is a lack of value placed on it, clearly signalled by the non-existent pay, because raising a family isn't seen as important or as a job or career. If your purpose is to create a loving, supportive environment for those around you and you do this by focusing on your family, then that is what matters to you and it is of great value. By owning our decisions in life outside the existing dominant value system and instead focusing on what we believe our personal purpose to be, we will feel more confident in them. That does not mean we shouldn't put pressure on governments to acknowledge the service stay-at-home parents are providing to society.

Living by your purpose frees you from the constraints of being defined by a job title or role. Formulating my purpose liberated me because I knew that no matter what I did – whether in this role or another – I was always going to focus on inspiring other women to find their fierce. Your job or job title becomes a means to an end, and that end is fulfilling your purpose.

But how to discover your purpose, when you've been conditioned all along to believe climbing a metaphorical career ladder is the most important thing? The answer is surprisingly simple, and lies within you: it is the moments you believe have shaped you as a person that will tell you who you are and what you want to stand for. Those life-defining episodes are often likely to be challenges or adversity that you have encountered and that have shaped you.

One of those moments in my own life was meeting a young woman called Beatrice. Let me tell you about her ...

Beatrice's story

Beatrice was 13 when I met her on the outskirts of Addis Ababa, the capital of Ethiopia. It was 2004 and I was director of programmes for Womankind Worldwide, an organisation that works in solidarity with women's movements and local women's groups to advance women's rights worldwide.[6] I was working on a project on early and forced marriage and female genital mutilation, supporting young girls along with another local organisation.

This was my first time in Ethiopia, one of the poorest countries in Africa. More than 80 per cent of the population lives in rural areas and relies on small farm plots for their livelihood. Disasters including droughts, floods, disease and conflict mean that many live in extreme poverty, especially women and children.

On my third day in the city, we drove for an hour down dusty roads to one of the villages just outside Addis Ababa, to visit communities where a local organisation was working with young girls.

When we arrived at the school, we went straight to one of the classrooms, where around 50 girls of all ages were being taught basic numeracy and literacy skills. When I say classroom, it was a room in a half-built structure that at one point was going to be a school but had never been finished. There was no glass in the windows, no paint on the walls. The girls did not have desks and shared basic wooden benches, crammed together in this relatively small room. But I could sense how excited and happy each girl was to be there.

Standing at the front of the class, I looked around at the faces of all these girls looking back at me. I felt moved and grateful to be there and to meet them. We connected without speaking. One thing I have learned through doing my work is that you can recognise and acknowledge each other just by seeing another person. I saw so many girls, all different, all with a different story.

But there was one who made me stop and look again. It was Beatrice. I could feel there was something very special about her. Everything about her screamed out that she had lived far beyond her years and had experienced more than any 13-year-old girl should ever have to. I asked whether she would be willing to talk to me. After class, with the help of a translator, we spoke. All the other girls had left and we were standing next to each other in front of one of the windows, overlooking the courtyard. And she told me her story.

Beatrice had her genitals cut when she was three. She remembered how painful it had been and how much she bled. The cutter had used a rusty razor blade, which had given her an infection. Due to complications, she leaked urine. The smell meant that Beatrice was shunned by others in the community.

When she was 11, Beatrice's family married her off to a 40-year-old man. She didn't want to get married, but her family was poor and needed the dowry they received – a cow. Beatrice's husband was violent towards her every day. He would drink, come home and rape her. She told me that she tried to escape early on and even once ran home to her family, but they sent her back, telling her that she no longer belonged to them, but instead was now the property of her husband. She would have had nowhere to go if it hadn't been for a woman in the village who took her in and allowed her to stay. This woman connected Beatrice to the organisation that Womankind Worldwide was supporting. They found her a home and enrolled her in their programme, teaching her basic numeracy and literacy skills.

When Beatrice finished her story, I could see the pain in her face. She had experienced unspeakable things that no one should ever have to.

For a split second, I lost all hope in humanity.

But there was Beatrice, standing next to me, aged 13, with the saddest story I had ever heard. I could not allow myself to sink into despair. I felt an urge to find a light in this darkness. Beatrice had entrusted her story to me and now I had to play my part. But I didn't know what that part was – none of this was happening in my rational mind, I was following my instincts.

I found myself looking at Beatrice and asking her: 'What are your dreams, Beatrice, what are you hoping for?'

The minute the question came out of my mouth I felt silly. How could I ask her such a stupid question, when she had been through so much? But as I was silently scolding myself, and the translator repeated my words, I saw Beatrice's face light up.

It was like a miracle.

Her face, which had carried deep sadness from the very moment I first saw her and all through her story, suddenly came alive and she smiled. I felt I was witnessing something impossible.

'I want to learn English.'

She wanted to learn English.

After all she had been through, her answer was so unexpected. It seemed so simple. I could not believe it. She wanted to learn English.

Beatrice showed me that what happens to us, no matter how horrendous the atrocities, does not have to define us or mean that we are victims. Not as long as we can find hope.

A year later, my colleague visited Beatrice and she was going to school regularly, living with the same woman, who had become like a family to her, and she was speaking English.

Beatrice inspired me deeply. Meeting her changed me in an intense, fundamental way. She strengthened my resolve to be true to my fierce and believe in myself and what I see as my role in life. Meeting her strengthened my purpose.

Of course, I was already passionate about helping women, but I knew from then on that I was always going to find hope – however deeply it was buried – and I was going to invest in it, because no matter what we might experience, **as long as we have hope, we can move from fears to fierce.**

The importance of formulating your purpose

Beatrice strengthened my resolve to be true to my fierce and trust myself. It wasn't until several years later, however, that

I found myself formulating my purpose statement during a workshop and realised that meeting Beatrice had given me such meaning. Often, it's only with hindsight that we can see the impact someone or something has had on us.

She had helped me find my purpose.

Here's the key: a purpose shouldn't be some nebulous thing you hold inside your head. I learned the power of writing down my purpose over a decade ago, during a seminar about leadership run by Aspire and Dr Sam Collins.[7] In that session, we each had to put our 'leadership purpose' down on paper.

My first thought was, 'That's ridiculous. There is no way I can do this for myself. How would that even work? And why? Anyway, I just can't see how it is going to change anything.' Even though I had a strong sense of purpose, I did not think of myself as having 'a purpose' and it had not occurred to me to write down what that purpose was.

I was worried I was simply not going to be able to do it, that I would make a fool of myself. I was fearful that I wasn't important enough to have a purpose and trying to write a purpose statement would make that really clear. This happens to us all: we are fearful to even try, because we worry that it will confirm that we are not good enough. Not trying somehow seems safer. The problem, of course, is that we will never know if we don't try.

Reading this, you might be feeling a similar sense of incredulity. Maybe you, like me, think you can't just sit down and create a purpose out of thin air. But what I learned through the workshop and my work since then is that it's not coming out of thin air, but you – your life, your experience. At the end of this chapter, I show you how to formulate your own purpose statement but, first, I'll tell you how I found mine.

I can honestly say that writing my purpose down all those years ago shifted something significant inside me. I remember

[7] www.aspirewomen.co.uk/index.php/about_aspire/dr_collins

the first time I told someone what my purpose was, using the phrase I had crafted at the seminar. As I listened to myself speak, I could hear a new resolve and certainty in my voice. And I noticed two things: firstly, I took myself more seriously and felt more sure of myself; and, secondly, the person I was speaking to was moved and inspired by my clarity and commitment.

Until then, I had been following my fierce, but I hadn't fully articulated it. But saying, 'Here is my purpose, this is what I am going to do with my life' is a brave, bold and hugely empowering thing to do. It gives your life and your actions meaning and clarity. You start to hold yourself accountable to your purpose. It's no longer someone else who evaluates and assesses you and determines your worth – it's you! You start to take full responsibility. This is the self-leadership I spoke about in the introduction.

Here's the thing: only you can do this for yourself. No one can give you your purpose. There are no ready-made purposes for sale or one-size-fits-all – you have to define it. That, though, is a wonderful thing, because if you create it, you own it. You'll be able to make decisions in your life informed by your purpose. Your decision and actions cease to be random; they become part of fulfilling your purpose and the impact you will have in the world.

The biggest shift for me? **My purpose was a validation of me – and my fierce – and it helped me see the road to living a different way.** Your purpose needs you to lead yourself for it to be fulfilled.

How I define my purpose

1. Reflect on life-changing moments and write them down

Looking back on moments in your life that have had an impact on you is a revealing exercise. It is often childhood memories[8] that are particularly powerful and reveal a lot about your fierce. As you know, moving to Venezuela and witnessing inequality set my fierce on fire.

I mentioned earlier in this chapter that it's the moments you believe have shaped you as a person that will tell you so much about who you are and what is important in your life. Those things will help you define your purpose. Here are the ones I identified and wrote down when I first did this:

> *The birth of my daughters*
> *My parents' divorce*
> *Receiving support and inspiration from a mentor*
> *My father asking me and not my brother to tidy the table*
> *Meeting Beatrice*

2. Consider what you have learned about yourself from each of those moments

This is not an easy exercise. When you do it yourself, give yourself time, because you will need to tune in to the pain you will inevitably uncover here. When I spoke about Beatrice, I said that where there is darkness, there is also light. Where there is pain, there is also the seed of happiness. That is what we are doing here.

I thought about why I remembered each moment and what I felt when I thought back to it, and wrote those feelings down too. Some questions I thought about were: who am I as a result? What did I learn from that experience? What are the values I formed as a result of the experience?

The moments I wrote down were all deeply challenging in a life-changing way. As I looked at them, I asked myself what I

---

[8] Nick Craig, president of the Authentic Leadership Institute, talks about this process in this short video: www.hbr.org/video/3479668068001/to-clarify-your-purpose-reflect-on-your-childhood

had taken from them that I carry with me now – other than the sense of them having been challenging. That is when I discovered that these experiences had shaped me in a profound way and defined my values.

There are three important points that I have reflected on since I did this exercise:

Firstly, if the experience is recent, you might not have enough distance from it, and this will make the exercise much harder, because you will have to sit with the pain for longer to be able to understand what the learning experience was.

Secondly, understanding the learning that comes from pain will not make the pain suddenly rosy. But though pain is pain, it can teach us something and we can learn to embrace it as part of life.

Finally, you might notice that I haven't labelled my feelings and experiences as positive or negative. How I perceive them might change over time, and what is negative for me might be positive for someone else. This exercise is about developing acceptance and understanding for what something is, not labelling it. **Understanding how something has shaped me is not about judging it – it just is.**

Let's go back to my example. The first life-changing moment I wrote down was:

The birth of my daughters:

> *What do I remember?*
> Pain, sadness, disappointment with myself.

Isn't that crazy? Of course, I also think of the births as the best moments of my life; there is nothing I love more than my daughters, and yet, if I am being really honest, I felt these emotions too.

I planned what the births of both my daughters were going to look like: water births at home without any medication.

Instead, I ended up in hospital both times for hours on end with all the drugs available. I was determined to breastfeed all the way, and with both of them, after three months, I had to give up because I was not producing enough milk. I had mastitis early on and both my daughters were not gaining the weight they needed. I was encouraged to supplement after the first month, which meant that gradually my daughters lost interest in breast milk. It broke my heart. I had failed. I was not good enough. It shook me profoundly. I felt disappointed in myself. I had been determined that I was going to do the whole 'mothering' thing so well and judged myself because I couldn't. Looking back now, I am sad at how harsh I was on myself.

What did I take from this experience?

Once I got through the pain of feeling like a failure, I was able to focus on what was important: that both my daughters were well – yes, even with drugs and without breastfeeding. I learned that I needed to relax, live in the moment, appreciate the now, really listen, loosen my attachment to expectations, be open to life unfolding. The experience laid the groundwork for practising unconditional trust in myself ... still, of course, a work in progress. More about trust in chapter 4.

My parents' divorce:

What do I remember?

Loss, pain, grief, sadness, fear, loneliness, disappointment, rejection, abandonment, anger.

My parents divorced when I was 22 and I still remember the searing sadness and trauma that I felt. I had believed in their relationship and losing that shook me deeply. It broke my heart and hope, for a while. It filled me with fear and scepticism for all relationships, and turned me violently against marriage. For years I would openly proclaim that I would never get married because, well, what would be the point? I guess it is surprising that, even at 22, a divorce can have that impact on you. I was already living on my own at university, so it didn't change my day-to-day. This was about the foundations I had attached myself to changing unexpectedly.

What did I take from this experience?

A commitment to loyalty, honesty, letting go and forgiving. After my parents' divorce, the need to commit overwhelmed me. I knew that if I committed, I would be very careful, because I would want to honour that commitment. I think that is why I am like a terrier; even if things are hard, I won't give up, I will stick at it. This time in my life also made me acutely aware of the responsibility we have as individuals to be mindful of how we influence the lives of others. I am committed to bearing this responsibility consciously and honouring it. At the same time, I don't want to judge my parents, as I don't know what went on in their lives. All I know is how I felt and what I learned from it and how it shaped me, which, in terms of my life and purpose, is all that matters. The more you make things make sense to yourself, the more whole you become.

Receiving support and inspiration from a mentor:

What do I remember?
Worry, self-doubt.

In 2004, I was promoted to manage the full programme portfolio for Womankind Worldwide, something I had never done before, and I knew I needed help. This was an incredible opportunity, but I was aware of the responsibility and I wanted to do it justice. I was worried and scared that I might not be able to rise to the challenge. I needed someone with expertise, whom I could trust, and who could support me on my journey.

That someone was Tina Wallace, a development researcher, teacher and gender adviser.[9] I had met her through my then boss, Maggie Baxter, who recommended her to me. I remember meeting Tina for the first time and being so inspired by her. Tina was special because she did not follow any conventions. I saw her as someone who didn't worry about what other people thought or said about her. She was going to speak her truth. She often openly challenged large institutions, calling out practices that were in stark contrast with their proclaimed values. At the same time, I had never met anyone who was more committed to listening properly, finding inclusive ways of talking to people, and learning. Tina became my guide for four years, supporting me, giving me space and helping me develop my own voice and thinking. She encouraged my passion for lifelong learning, questioning the status quo and not resting on assumptions.

Who am I as a result?

I follow my passion, my instincts and my thoughts. Tina gave me permission to be me. It was enough for her that I showed up with my ears, my eyes, my brain and my fierce. I didn't know my fierce then half as well as I do now, but it was there and Tina, in everything she did, encouraged it! Her belief in me gave me more confidence and resolve to trust myself and know that I am enough.

My father asking me and not my brother to tidy the table:

What do I remember?
Outrage, anger, deep feeling of injustice, rage.

You know this story from chapter 1. The memory always comes to my mind immediately when I think about moments in my

[9] www.lmh.ox.ac.uk/igs/academic-community/research-associates-and-junior-research-associates/tina-wallace

childhood that have formed me. My commitment to equality stems from my own experience of inequality but also from witnessing its impact on others.

Meeting Beatrice:

> *What do I remember?*
> Despair, sadness, hope.

You know that meeting Beatrice changed my life. Sometimes you meet people in your life who touch you so deeply you will never forget them, and Beatrice was one of those people for me. She touched my fierce in a profound way and what I took from that moment was a commitment to courage, hope and believing that change is possible even in the darkest moments.

3. Organise the words into two lists

On one side I put the words that described the experience and on the other I wrote the words that described who I am as a result. Sometimes the opposite meaning of a word can clarify your values. For example, insensitivity is something that makes me sad; I don't understand it. The opposite of insensitivity is compassion, which is close to my purpose.

Next, I circled the words that resonated with me the most. These were on my list:

> *Commitment to equality*
> *Fairness*
> *Justice*
> *Hope*
> *Compassion*
> *Passion*
> *Standing up for what you believe in*
> *Respect*
> *Fulfilling your potential*

4. Writing your purpose statement

Using the words I had identified throughout this process, I wrote a sentence that summed up what I'd learned about myself. My first version read like this:

> *I am a leader who is strong, loyal and committed to equality and passionate about enabling/allowing everyone to live their life to the full for the sake of a happier organisation helping more women, ending war and building peace.*

I then redrafted this statement at least TEN times and ended up with this:

> *I am a leader who believes in her convictions. I am strong, loyal and committed to equality and justice. I am passionate about enabling people to reach their potential for the sake of empowering more women, ending war and building peace.*

About a year ago, I redrafted it:

> *My purpose is to inspire other women to fulfil their dreams and their potential in order to create a more just and happy world filled with love.*

It might strike you that in my first purpose statement I started with 'I am a leader'. Why? The answer goes to the heart of why I wanted to write *Fears to Fierce*. We still confine ourselves to believing that we only need a purpose if we are a 'leader' in a professional capacity. The seminar I went to ten years ago took us through an exercise of defining our 'leadership purpose' and it was focused on our work and how we would be better, stronger leaders at our organisations or businesses. But I have since realised that this limited understanding of leadership does not serve us as humans. Being in a leadership role at work does not make you a leader.

Leading your life with commitment to your fierce? Now that is the kind of leadership that serves us well. Therefore, **our purpose is not just about who we are at work. It is about all of who we are.** It needs to work for us in all areas of our life. It goes back to what I said earlier about focusing on purpose over career. My purpose now works for me at work, at home, with my friends. It might be **my 'leadership' purpose, but the person I am leading is ME!** As I said in the introduction, when I talk about leadership, I mean self-leadership. You can inspire others to lead themselves, but you are not leading anyone else but you (more about this in chapter 3).

And as you lead yourself, you transform. As you transform, you might want to revisit your purpose. That is good. Your purpose statement is not a straitjacket – it is there for you, to help you and remind you of your way and why you are going in that direction. Since I first formulated my purpose statement, I have changed it several times. With every change, I feel I come closer to my essence, which is exciting. My latest one is:

My purpose is to inspire other women to find their FIERCE in order to create a more peaceful world filled with love.

Remember, your purpose statement does not have to be perfect. It can evolve over time and it is just for you! Only you get to determine your purpose statement and whether it is serving you.

You are not alone

Leading yourself can get lonely. But if you pay attention to the people around you who move you, you'll meet others with similar purposes. They will inspire you. And inspiration, as we know from chapter 1, ignites our fierce and gives us the strength to focus on our purpose. Getting into the habit of reflecting on what it is that resonates with you when you hear something that inspires you will strengthen your commitment to your purpose. That is why I asked you at the end of chapter 1 to create habits for inspiration.

Defining, following and owning your purpose takes courage every day. It requires strong self-leadership, so in the next chapters you'll get to focus on how to cultivate it for yourself.

Lessons learned

We all have our own unique purpose.

Having a purpose means that your decisions and actions become part of a bigger picture.

Your purpose gives your life and actions meaning and clarity.

Your purpose is a commitment to your self-leadership.

Your purpose validates you and your fierce.

Your purpose acknowledges life-changing moments that have made you who you are.

You can change and adjust your purpose as you transform.

Your purpose is yours alone; no one gets to judge it.

Actions

Now it's time to formulate your own purpose statement. It doesn't have to be perfect – mine certainly wasn't at first, and I still change it whenever I want!

You can use my process outlined in this chapter to help guide the development of your own purpose and purpose statement, but these are the steps in brief:

Define your purpose

Sit down and answer the following questions in writing:

- What events have had a key impact on your life?

- Reflect on what you have learned about yourself from these key events. Why do you remember that moment? What do you feel when you think back to it? Write down the feelings – it doesn't have to be long sentences, words are fine. Who are you as a result? What did you learn from that experience? What are the values that you formed as a result of the experience?

- Have a look at the list of words that you have written. Organise them into two lists so that on one side you have the words that describe the experience, and on the other you have the words that describe who you are as a result.

- Circle the words that resonate the most with you, the ones you love!

- Write your own purpose statement.

Practise your purpose

- Share your purpose statement with someone else. This will most likely feel a little bit uncomfortable, which is all the more reason to do it! Articulating your purpose statement to someone else will reinforce its power. You can tell a friend about it, or a colleague, anyone, it doesn't matter. You can tell them about the process or you can just weave it into the conversation without telling them that it's a big deal for you.

- Reflect on how you feel having shared your purpose.

- Pin it up in a place where you'll see it regularly. Since your statement will be new to you, it is a good reminder and will help you to become more comfortable with it.

- Revisit it as and when you want – don't forget, this is a process!

- Make thinking about your purpose a habit. You are shifting your mindset and that needs practice. Think about the power of your purpose, what it means to you and how it can help you to look at opportunities differently.

- Make speaking about your purpose a habit. This will help you with shifting your mindset and with becoming comfortable with your purpose. The more you think and speak about it, the more it will guide your thoughts and actions.

- Be inspired by other purposeful self-leaders. Think about people you know who seem like they have a clear purpose. They can be people you personally know or public figures. Oprah Winfrey, for example, is a strong purpose-driven individual. Many of the people Oprah interviews on her *SuperSoul Sundays* podcast are also purpose-driven. Once you start following one, it will be easy to connect to others.

- Add a purposeful leader to the boardroom in your heart. They will be there to remind you of your purpose when you need it.

- Let me know your thoughts about the process and how you found it. @BritaFS

PART II

Own Your Power

Chapter 3

Power

You are the hero of your story

'Maybe Eve was never meant to be our warning. Maybe she was meant to be our model.
Own your wanting.
Eat the apple.
Let it burn.'

– Glennon Doyle[10]

Lead yourself like you are enough

What holds us back from leading ourselves?

FEAR! Of course.
The fear that we are not enough.
The fear that we are not strong enough.
The fear that we are not lovable.
The fear that we are too broken.

Over many years of working with wonderful humans around the world and reflecting on my own life, I have seen how fear holds us back from uncovering our potential and fulfilling our purpose. As a result, I have concluded that nurturing four key

[10] Glennon Doyle, *Untamed* (Vermilion, 2020)

elements – **trust, strength, love** and **care** – needs to be at the heart of leading ourselves. Those four pillars are the focus of the next four chapters.

These words sound simple but they are incredibly challenging when you apply them to yourself. Yes, this part of the book is all about you! We'll be talking about how trusting YOURSELF, realising YOUR strength, loving YOURSELF and caring for YOURSELF are all key if you want to own your power. Our aim is to lead ourselves knowing that we are enough, and we'll begin to believe it if we cultivate these elements.

This is where *fears to fierce* will need to become a mantra for you, because we are going to dig deep into fear. But we are going to go step-by-step, with practical exercises you can use as you go. The process of owning your power will start with redefining how you value yourself and reclaiming your agency. You will learn how to draw the line, change your self-talk and make friends with your ego. All of this will grow a deep trust right within you. The next step is to understand how our fear that we are not strong enough to withstand pain paralyses us. Knowing that you are stronger than you think in all aspects of your life allows you to embrace your fierce. My favourite part is that you then get to practise and nurture LOVE. I will guide you to get out of your head and into your heart, finding love all around you. Finally, you will get to decide how to care for yourself. These four pillars are interconnected and interlinked. They mutually reinforce each other and together embolden your fierce.

'In-powerment' not 'empowerment'

While the first part of the fears to fierce journey focused on being inspired and articulating your purpose, this next stage is about owning your power so that you feel brave enough to act.

Owning your power is often referred to as 'empowerment'; a term that has been overused to the point where it means everything and nothing. I want to spend a moment explaining why I choose to express it differently. Empowerment is often understood as something that is given to us or done to us. Sometimes, particularly when there's the need for structural changes that define where power is held, such as the right to vote, power is indeed 'given'. But for this to lead to change, we must realise that the power to be active agents is within us, because only we can 'empower' ourselves. This requires us to be 'in' our power, which is why I believe **'in-powerment' is a more accurate description for the process by which we come to truly own our power. Your power already resides within you; no one else can give it to you.**

In order to believe that we have this power, it is helpful to rethink how we understand 'leadership'. I have already spoken about how people inspire us by 'leading' themselves and standing up for their purpose. In this way, 'in-powerment' is a continuation of what you began when you defined your purpose because self-leadership is the catalyst for everything else you'll do. If inspiration ignites your fierce and motivates you to formulate your purpose, is inspiration not then the greatest impact any of us can have? As you lead yourself, you will inspire those around you to do that for themselves.

Self-leadership

I grew up believing that I should strive to be a leader, particularly in relation to my 'career'. I believed that leaders were strategic and special, that not everyone could be one. Only certain people would make it to the top, where they could then be called *leaders*. 'Do I have what it takes to be a leader?' I would worry, having fully bought into this notion.

There are many assumptions and stereotypes about leadership, and these are often based on patriarchal notions of organising the world, where a few exceptional (and who defines that?) individuals are leaders, and they have all the *power*. But as I inched closer to a leadership role in my own career, I realised that I didn't identify with this definition of 'leadership'.

I worked for gender equality causes, and I saw that this notion of 'leadership' was perpetuating inequality. I understood that I needed to challenge the idea that power is held in the hands of a few (mainly) men – and that women needed to prove themselves worthy to crack the glass ceiling so that a *few* of us would also have power. I wasn't looking for 'top-down' leadership, where power is in the hands of a few and people follow them. I wanted a different approach, which championed the idea that we all have power within us.

We are all leaders

Traditional hierarchies value people according to their material possessions or job titles, but these things don't tell us anything about who people are as human beings. When we look deeper and strip 'leaders' of traditional notions of power, leadership suddenly becomes something different. It no longer seems so out of reach.

In fact, we're all leading our own lives. Without realising, we lead ourselves every day. Whether we like it or not, whether we aspire to or not, we take actions and make choices that have an impact. When we acknowledge our agency in this way, we come closer to realising that we have the ability to shape our lives. It requires us to take back the power that we so often give up. When you begin owning your power, you lead yourself.

The first step towards 'in-powering' ourselves is exactly as the word suggests – **realising that the power is within us**. No matter where we are in the world, what we might have gone through, how much or how little money we have, we do have power and we do get to decide if or how we use it.

Don't give it up, deny it or ignore it. Many of us wait for others to tell us how to 'succeed', rather than defining what 'success' looks like for ourselves. We follow other people's ideas, often without questioning, and do what we believe is expected. We forget to really listen to our fierce.

Even small acts of taking back your power embody the self-leadership I'm talking about. One of the most important elements of the Women for Women International programme is that women are asked to decide whether they *want* to enrol. The focus is on their decision-making; it is not presented as a handout, or a quick fix for a 'victim', but acknowledges women as agents of change both in their own lives and more broadly. It embraces the notion of self-leadership and it is this self-leadership that is the trigger for wider societal changes, something that we will explore later in the book.

Trust the process

Owning your power is a process and, as you go through the fears to fierce journey, you might find that your sense of integrity shifts. I used to think of 'integrity' as something made up of a set of values that are constant and unchanging which you acted according to – always. I realise now that this definition of integrity was one I needed to give me security. Now, I see integrity more like a membrane; it is alive and evolves as we grow. I think Robert E. Quinn, in his book *Deep Change*, puts it best when he says we '[build] integrity through the constant observation of one's lack of integrity'. Melis Senova, a wonderful woman, human-centred design expert and executive coach, with whom I worked a few years ago, refers to the same concept but in the context of design integrity: when you interrogate design and it makes sense and holds true, it has design integrity. I have adopted that interpretation: my integrity moves, but at any point in time you can interrogate me from every angle and I will make sense. I don't use my shifting integrity to punish myself, or to hold myself up to unreachable standards.

A good example of that is my purpose. As you know, when I first formulated my purpose statement, it read quite differently to how it reads now. Before I embraced the notion that as you change, your integrity changes – which now makes so much sense that it seems strange I ever thought otherwise – I would have considered that changing my purpose statement was a weakness, a sign I wasn't committed. I had a strong sense that to have integrity, I had to be steadfast and stick to my word no matter what. Instead, I now embrace change, and I don't see changing my views and therefore what I say, 'my word', as being feeble. It just is what it is: change. As I change, so does my integrity.

Do you sometimes feel you are changing so much that some of the things you proclaimed as eternal truths for yourself are now no longer so? Allow yourself to evolve and change your mind. It is all part of the process. If you look at yourself with those new views and values and they make sense to you, that is what matters. In that way, you always have integrity, because you make sense to yourself. And if you feel you don't make sense to yourself, then fear not: the next few chapters will help you get to know yourself better!

Fear as we transform

As you embark on this next part, there will be moments when you feel elated and overcome with gratitude at the realisation that you are ENOUGH, that you are the perfect leader for your purpose – because you are. As you uncover the root of your fear, you will heal wounds and find joy. But as is so often the case, alongside the elation, there will be fear. Fear that this feeling might not last, that perhaps feeling so 'in-powered' is a fluke, but don't worry. Recognise the fear and trust yourself, begin to know that **you can feel fear *and* choose your fierce simultaneously. Breathe. Let go of the fear. Keep going.** You are changing a lifetime's worth of habits, beliefs and attitudes, and this will take time.

The process of getting to know yourself and understanding why you might give away or distrust your power will mean facing your fears head-on. You will encounter testing situations where you will have to choose between feeling fear and giving into it, or looking at the fear, tapping into your fierce and leading yourself on your terms.

You are whole

Owning my power has forced me to discover different parts of myself and has allowed me to embrace what seem like opposites – cruelty and kindness, darkness and light, pride and shame, joy and pain, love and anger. Nurturing my self-leadership has allowed me to embrace those contradictions within me as part of who I am. It has made me feel whole, rather than seeing the co-existence of those binaries as proof that I was broken or messed up. I was able to let go of the limiting definitions of what others might see as whole, and define what wholeness means to me.

Your leadership is yours and yours alone; no one else needs to validate it or tell you that you are doing well. But, as with your purpose statement, don't use the concept of self-leadership to create an idealised version of yourself that you'll use to punish yourself. If you do that, you'll replace one straitjacket with another.

In the next four chapters, I will share with you stories of how broken I felt, how I became mentally and physically exhausted, how I doubted myself and how I found my way home to my fierce, to a place where I am whole. This is a place where I belong, where I lead my life in a way that helps me fulfil my purpose. If you commit to this, there will be moments of magic, where you feel connected to your fierce and what really matters to you. It's like training a muscle; sometimes it gets so hard that you want to give up, and then you'll have a breakthrough. **You'll feel like you have grown from the inside** to become stronger, calmer, more focused. Through leading and committing to yourself, you lose fear and you embrace your fierce.

Lessons learned

Think of empowerment as 'in-powerment'; a process by which you own the power within you.

As you lead yourself, you inspire those around you to lead themselves. We are all leaders.

Self-leadership means taking responsibility for ourselves.

Self-leadership is the trigger for wider societal changes.

Trust, strength, love and care are the key pillars for your self-leadership.

Actions

Take a deep breath and say: 'I am excited, ready and committed to my journey of "in-powerment".' You may also want to set a few intentions for this part of the book:

- **ALLOW** whatever comes up over the next few chapters.

- **ACCEPT** that change takes time. Be patient with yourself.

- **ACKNOWLEDGE** your progress, your learning, your 'aha' moments.

- **ASK** for help if this is hard. We can be scared of the 'truth' inside of ourselves. You don't have to endure in silence or solitude.

Write your intentions down in your own words, adding others if they come to mind. Above all, be open to venturing deep within yourself in your quest to reconnect with your amazing power!

Chapter 4

Trust

You are enough, so trust yourself unconditionally

'When we keep choosing right or wrong, we spend our life sorting rather than living. It doesn't mean that there aren't things that are cruel, or unjust, but only from the wholeness of life can we see how the spirit navigates.'

– Mark Nepo[11]

'Am I a good girl?'

It's a small question, perhaps, but my struggle to answer it held me captive for such a long time. It became central to the inner tug-of-war occurring between my fierce, my passion for justice and equality, and my fear that I wouldn't be accepted and liked if I followed those instincts.

When I think about where it came from and why I gave it so much power, I invariably end up at the point in my life when my family and I moved to Venezuela. Being a 'good girl' meant, to my teenage mind, being demure, submissive, likeable, and not talking back or disagreeing – especially not with my father. It definitely didn't mean being loud or voicing my opinion. Fitting into this system involved responding to the expectations and

---

[11] Mark Nepo in conversation with Oprah Winfrey, *SuperSoul Sundays* podcast

needs of others, even if they weren't what I needed, and bowing to the gender stereotypes ruling our society.

So often, I have found the desire to be liked coming into direct conflict with my fierce, and this has created an exhausting internal battle. When we live our lives in a way which we – deep down – know to be inauthentic, we lose trust in ourselves, because we doubt what is within us and place value on other people's – and society's – views. Forced to conclude that we can't be fully fierce and fully liked creates a rupture within us, trying to please both sides, without even realising. When we don't fully trust ourselves, part of us is always going to be ruled by a fear of what other people think. We don't embrace opportunities – we probably don't even see them – and we reject change. We become stuck in a kind of personal purgatory, a paralysis.

That is, until you start your fears to fierce journey. When you want to transform from within, what you're also saying is that you want to find a way back to trusting yourself. When we trust ourselves, and I mean really trust ourselves, we experience a profound shift that makes everything else – the strength, love and care I'll talk about in the next few chapters – possible.

Having supported women all over the world, I know that you can only 'in-power' yourself if you trust yourself – it's as simple as that! So how can we nurture that deep and unconditional self-trust?

First: Question the questions

Let's look closer at the questions that have led us to silence our fierce and held us in fear. For me, some of those were:

Am I good enough?
Am I strong enough?
Am I clever enough?
Am I pretty enough?
Am I liked enough?

You can add other examples that have held you captive.

Implicit in these questions is that a) we are not already enough, and b) somewhere there exists an exact measurement of what being enough means that was defined by someone else.

In this way, we are conditioned to give away agency and passively await our fate. Someone else will decide if we are clever, beautiful, strong, good, likeable or NOT. We are held captive by an authority we don't know and don't question. And, to make matters worse, we have no idea when these questions will be answered. They all point to a future self and remind us that we are most certainly none of this yet – and might never be. I believe these things to be at the heart of why we are too fearful to trust ourselves.

But when we interrogate the assumptions that hold us back, we begin questioning the questions:

Enough for WHAT?
Enough for WHOM?

We live by measurements that we do not understand. We have given away agency. And we live in a future beyond our control.

Once I stopped and I realised all of this, I knew that if I was ever going to be able to trust myself, I needed to be the one deciding what 'good enough' meant and I needed to allow myself to live right now, rather than in a future I didn't know.

This conditioning has been going on for centuries. It is part of our DNA, so it's not going to be easy to unpick.

Redefine how you value yourself

The good, the bad and the ugly

If you want to learn to trust yourself, you'll need to accept your whole self – the good, bad and ugly – because none of us are 100 per cent one thing. This is the part where we say goodbye to the binary value systems that deem things 'good' or 'bad', and embrace a messy medley, where perfection is not something to strive for.

I learned this lesson quite a few years ago, at work. A colleague was treating me badly – it took me a while to admit it, but the person was bullying me. It wasn't constant or exclusively directed at me, but when under pressure the person would speak loudly, using menacing words and intimidating behaviour in the belief that this would make me more likely to do what they were asking. They would instinctively find people's vulnerabilities and use them to undermine and cajole.

When I felt strong, I was able to recognise that this behaviour resulted from the person's own insecurities and I felt compassion and tried to help and support them. I knew not to take it personally. But the longer the situation continued, and as the person's actions became more frequent, the harder it was to bear. Not taking it personally became more difficult. Increasingly, their comments would trigger the desired effect in me, leading me to question myself.

I sensed this wasn't right and didn't understand why no one stopped it. This was at a time when I was not the most senior person in the workplace. I considered challenging this person's unacceptable behaviour myself; after all, it was in such contrast to my values. But I didn't want to cause trouble.

The situation played into my deepest fears of not being a 'good girl'. I didn't want to whistle-blow because I wanted to be compassionate, and I also worried about what people would think of me – 'Brita is just exaggerating … ', 'Brita is too demanding; no one can please her … ', and so went the story in my head. I let my fears outweigh my fierce. I didn't trust myself, and as a result I was not being true to my own value system.

Then one day, it came to a head. I had made a mistake and the person got angry about it – angry in a way that was not justified. I had forgotten to consult with them on something, and they just flipped. They said unacceptable and hurtful things to me. They questioned my professional behaviour and commitment to the organisation. They threatened me. They told me that no one would respect me, that they were going to make sure everyone knew about my error, and that I would pay. They accused me of being motivated more by a desire to be seen, than to benefit the organisation. My heart was racing and my hands shook. It was awful.

But moments where we realise our biggest fears are also our greatest teachers.

Suddenly, the paralysis that had plagued me evaporated. The fear and pain of the hurtful words were so strong that it made me wake up. I thought two things: firstly, I knew that if the person had talked like this to someone else, I would do something to stop it. Secondly, if someone spoke to one of my daughters like that, I would hope she would defend herself. I realised that not standing up for my values, living by the values of others because of fear, was directly opposed to my purpose and what really mattered to me in my life. And so I decided it was time to tap into my fierce. I took a moment to calm myself. Then I decided to confide in someone who I trusted and ask for help. I developed an action plan outlining the steps I would take to formally complain about the situation.

The following few weeks were a journey of tapping into the fierce values that I hold dear but had given up on. I relearned how to use those values to value myself. At the time I wrote in my journal:

> *The fear I feel is not about the external consequences of losing my job; it's the fear that I am not worthy – that I don't deserve to be strong, stand up for my values and say, 'It's not okay to treat me like this.'*

It made me think back to my childhood. Had I learned then that I had to cope with situations that I didn't think were right but had no means to affect? Had I decided what was happening to me was my fault because I hadn't been a 'good girl'? Did I therefore deserve to be punished? This long-held belief was keeping me prisoner and didn't allow me to embrace myself wholly – mistakes and all. It didn't allow me to believe that I was good enough. It stopped me from trusting myself.

Once I understood the origins of why I was feeling like this, I was able to change. I realised that I had to trust myself *even* when I had made a mistake, *even* when I had not been 'perfect'. That I *was* 'good' enough and I did deserve kindness, empathy and self-compassion.

I started a journey towards accepting all of who I am, the good, the bad and the ugly. As painful as it was, the experience healed a far deeper pain that is now gone because I felt like I was finding my way back to my authentic self. I came to trust myself and not external forces or expectations. Embracing all of me has given me a sense of wholeness.

- How do you value yourself?
- Do you accept parts of you that you don't like so much?
- What do your 'good', bad' and 'ugly' look like?
- How do you feel when you think of accepting the bad and the ugly?
- Can you pretend you are your best friend – does that help you to accept yourself fully?
- If you are struggling with this, ask yourself why?

Inspecting beliefs

Another way of describing the journey I went on is as a process of interrogating the deep-seated beliefs I held about myself. The key one? That I was not worthy of respect if I made a mistake. Writing it down like that sounds easy, pithy. But journeying to that realisation was not easy at all. Questioning why we believe we are not good enough, then letting those beliefs go and replacing them with a new conviction, is at the heart of redefining how we value ourselves and developing trust.

Executive coach Melis Senova says: 'Beliefs are like operating systems. They are the framework for how we experience life.' We therefore need to examine how our beliefs impact our ability to trust ourselves. As I was doing this work, I realised I had formed most of my beliefs as a response to an event; something that happened to me that I needed to make sense of and led me to believe certain things about myself. Others I had been told and accepted them as truths.

This is what I mean when I talk about redefining our value system. We get to examine our beliefs and decide if we like them. If they don't serve us, we let them go, and replace them with other beliefs that serve us better on our journey.

When I was being bullied, I came to believe that I deserved to be treated badly, even though I did not think bullying was acceptable. But after I saw that I was not the only one suffering, I replaced those beliefs with the conviction that I had the same right as everyone else not to be bullied. This process requires trust in ourselves and it also builds trust ... like an upward spiral where we are constantly reinforcing ourselves. We get to choose the measures by which we value our worth. We determine what the best version of ourselves looks like.

Another belief I held close, so close it took me a while to realise it was a belief and not a fact, was: *I am not creative.* I would weave this into my narrative casually like stating a fact – 'I'll ask someone to come up with an idea for this project, because I am not creative.' I didn't beat myself up about it. In fact, I felt quite grown up – like I knew my strengths, and creativity wasn't one of them. And that was fine.

A few years ago, I was forced to revisit this deep-seated belief. My daughters were 12 and 14. One of them said, 'I won't be any good at that', as a fact, just as I always said I wasn't creative. I was taken aback and realised that my creativity belief directly contradicted another of my beliefs: we must not ever think we cannot do something before we have tried. I'm passionate about this belief because it links directly to my purpose of helping others uncover their potential, so I obviously needed to revisit the assumptions I'd made about my artistic instincts! How could I convince my daughter to trust her ability unconditionally and have a go at everything if I didn't trust myself in the same way?

I came to understand that I had defined creativity in a narrow way. I can't draw particularly well, so I'd written off 'creativity' altogether. To change this belief, I looked for tools to help me unravel it. One was Elizabeth Gilbert's book *Big Magic*. She makes a powerful case for the fact that we are all creative, if we believe it: *'If you're alive, you're a creative person.'*[12] Reading her book liberated me from my limiting belief that I wasn't creative. Changing beliefs doesn't happen overnight. It takes time, dedication and practice. But it is possible – and I no longer say I'm not creative.

Doing 'beliefs work' invites us to see that we have the capacity to change from within. But we can only change what we know, so it is also a journey of getting to know ourselves. There will be beliefs that serve us that we want to keep. Those that limit us from uncovering our potential, following our purpose and trusting ourselves we reconsider. This is deep work, so I have included an exercise to help you inspect your beliefs at the end of this chapter.

Overhauling how you value yourself by questioning the beliefs you've accepted as facts about yourself is not something you can do quickly, so don't rush and, above all, be kind to yourself. You are undoubtedly going to uncover some things that are hard to face. I know from myself and the women I have worked with that the 'truth' inside ourselves can be scary. I imagine taking myself by the hand and saying: 'We've got this. We are going to be fine.' **Once you define your own value system, you're in the driving seat on the road to freedom where you are no longer held captive by the expectations of others.** You get to decide that you are enough.

[12] Elizabeth Gilbert, *Big Magic* (Bloomsbury, 2016)

Reclaim your agency

The second step in the process of developing trust in ourselves is reclaiming our agency.

Now that you have rediscovered your values and recommitted to your fierce, you are ready to stand up for those values. The act of defending your values inspires deep trust, because through our actions we are showing ourselves how seriously we take our values, and therefore ourselves. Think about it: what makes us trust someone else? Often, it's because you see them being true to themselves and acting on their values.

Draw the line

When I was being bullied at work, I learned that if something or someone is violating your boundaries, you have to speak up, because only you know when they have been violated. You cannot wait for someone else to do this for you. **You are the guardian of your boundaries**.

So how did I gather the strength to stand up for myself when I hadn't done so before? It was the knowledge that this behaviour was also affecting others and the realisation that by not speaking out I was complicit; it wasn't that *I* endured pain, but that my silence was allowing this culture of fear to spread. **I was compromising my integrity. I was being disloyal to my purpose. I wasn't acting with agency.** This is why developing a strong and clear sense of your purpose is so powerful.

I didn't immediately react, instead giving myself time to sit with the pain and the uncomfortable feeling. I told myself that I trusted myself, that I accepted responsibility for the mistake I had made and that I had made peace with it. Still, the way I had been treated was not justified, and I had the right to put up clear boundaries and to signal when they had been crossed. I prepared and planned my course of action and asked for help and advice from a lawyer and a trusted friend. When I felt ready,

I spoke out, explaining why I was issuing a formal complaint, how it was linked to the values of the organisation and how I didn't want to accept such treatment. I leaned on my values to claim my agency. It felt like a test to see how true I was going to be to my new resolve to trust myself unconditionally. That helped; I felt I had made a promise to myself and I didn't want to break it.

I accepted that I didn't have to be perfect to demand boundaries. *We* determine our worth, nobody else.

This is worth repeating: **We determine our worth, nobody else.**

As I reclaim my agency, I no longer wait for someone else to tell me if I am good enough. I have a deep, unwavering trust in my whole self. My presence right now, here, is enough.

Self-talk

Because I had made a mistake and wasn't 'right', there was a part of me that thought I deserved the bad treatment and didn't have the right to speak out. I was trapped in the binary polarities of good and bad. I scolded myself and told myself off, blaming myself for the situation. I was harsh on myself. But life happens in the murky bits, the shades of grey, so what we need to do is sense our way through it with trust, kindness and self-compassion, knowing that we are enough, and deserve to be treated with respect.

How we speak to ourselves really matters. Jean Houston, in her book *The Wizard of Us*, explains how neuroplasticity shows us how the brain adapts and changes according to what we tell it: ' ... we could absolutely engage in self-directed neuroplasticity by taking time out each day to consciously replace the negative tapes that we may have been playing with thoughts of happiness, love, and wisdom'.[13]

[13] Jean Houston, *The Wizard of Us* (Atria Books, 2016)

Imagine if you spoke to yourself like you would speak to a person you care for, a person you trust, respect and love. Imagine that when you make a mistake, instead of telling yourself off, you say: 'I love you, you tried, you did your best, you made a mistake and now you can learn something from this experience. I know you've got this, because you are stronger than you think.' That feels completely different and opens up space for trust.

Practising self-compassion is an important and wonderful thing, but it will feel uncomfortable at the beginning. As Don Miguel Ruiz encourages us to do in his book, *The Four Agreements*, being impeccable with your word in your own mind and in what you say out loud about yourself is important. No more 'I am so stupid ... I am such an idiot ... ' Even if you don't really mean it, some of its insidious power will seep into your psyche. Replace these attacks on yourself with more affirmative words: saying 'I tried and this didn't work' makes a big difference to how you are going to feel about the situation.

Next time when you forget to do something, pay attention to what you say to yourself in your head. Make a commitment NOT to scold yourself. Perhaps laugh and tell yourself it's fine, it doesn't matter. It is hard to trust someone who is constantly telling you off, right? That is why it is so important that you take care with how you speak to yourself if you want to grow trust in yourself.

Once you start paying attention to words, you might feel mortified by how often you put yourself down. But it is in our power to change this. We can pay attention to our language and become more self-compassionate as we build trust in ourselves.

Kristin Neff speaks about self-compassion in her TED talk,[14] where she says that being kind to ourselves is a way of connecting with our shared humanity, practising love, warmth and caring, and mindfulness. **Nurturing self-compassion is therefore a pre-condition for creating a better world around you.**

[14] *The Space Between Self Esteem & Self Compassion*: Kristin Neff at TEDxCentennialParkWomen

Hello, ego, my old friend . . .

Throughout this process, your ego will cause havoc. You need to get to know and make friends with it in order to nurture trust in yourself.

As I mentioned, my colleague instinctively knew that I could be made to feel hurt by accusing me of serving my ego and not the workplace. They sensed that one of my deepest fears is that I am driven by my ego rather than my purpose, that I abuse my power in the service of my ego. What is important here is that **we all have an ego that is unique to us and it is important that we get to know it**. If we don't, we cannot be aware of how it is driving us, which in turn means we run the risk of following our ego rather than our values. This then interferes with trusting ourselves, because we don't understand our actions.

For a long time, my goal was to be free of my ego. I associated people with egos with being boisterous show-offs, while those who were humble and grateful, I thought, did not have an ego.

I have spent a lot of time thinking about and observing my ego and have learned that the ego thrives on pride, shame, guilt and fear. I believe we each have a series of triggers that can be traced back to one or more of those four key feelings.

Do you remember a time when someone gave you negative feedback and you thought: 'Who do they think they are?' This is a perfect example of the ego triggering your pride. In that moment, you have a choice. You can take a deep breath and realise your ego is triggered by feelings of pride, stop, let it go, and decide how you *really* want to respond to the feedback (and I'll bet it's calmly!). Or you can go down the rabbit hole and be outraged, and continue, 'Do they think they are better than me? Did they not mess up just last week?' And on, and on.

When we are being triggered, our ego lures us in and, if we allow it, it will dictate our behaviour and interfere with the trust we are trying to cultivate in ourselves.

I know that thinking about this is like doing brain acrobatics but understanding how it works is liberating. Knowing how to distinguish your ego from your fierce essence creates a pause, and in that space you'll find a way to manage those ego-driven feelings. Most of us are on a rollercoaster, reacting to thoughts, emotions and experiences directed by our ego, constantly forming attachments to idealised versions of ourselves and our lives. When you recognise your ego in action and let go of those attachments, you free yourself and embrace the possibility of just being YOU.

One image of myself that is incredibly important to me and therefore opens me up to enormous triggers is being a 'good mother'.

Even though I had wanted to be open-minded about being a mother, I quickly became attached to what a good pregnancy, healthy birth and perfect breastfeeding experience would look like if I were a 'good' parent, based on the advice given to me by others. This of course meant that when things turned out differently, I labelled them as 'wrong' or 'bad' and judged myself.

When Jose Luis and I found out that I was four weeks pregnant in 2000, we were so excited that we took photos with the pregnancy test and immediately called our families, proceeding to tell everyone our happy news. But when I told one friend that I was four weeks pregnant, she said that I shouldn't be telling anyone because there was a 30 per cent chance I would lose my baby in the first trimester. I looked this up and found that it was true: up to 25 per cent of pregnancies don't progress past the first twelve weeks.[15]

I felt foolish: my ego told me that I didn't really know what I was doing, and at the same time I was consumed by a fear that I would lose my baby. 'I am so stupid,' I thought, 'I should have known that you don't tell anyone about your pregnancy until you are at least three months pregnant.' My ego was wounded,

[15] www.tommys.org/our-organisation/charity-research/pregnancy-statistics/miscarriage

and sparked those egotistical emotions: pride, fear, shame and guilt because I had been caught out as someone who didn't know 'the rules' of parenthood. I could have stepped back, realised that being so harsh on myself was not helping me in any way, extended compassion to myself and trusted myself to be able to respond to whatever was going to happen, but I didn't.

Fast-forward to the birth. We wanted a home birth, no medication, natural. You may remember I told you about this as one of my defining moments that helped me formulate my purpose. I hadn't left any room for life's messy bits and, of course, the birth didn't adhere to my grand plan. Emma was born in hospital and during labour I'd accepted pain relief. Of course, our daughter being healthy was the most important thing, but what I now know to be my ego also made me feel guilty and ashamed. It was the same with breastfeeding: I assumed that in order to be a 'great' parent, I needed to master breastfeeding, but I had to stop completely when Emma was three months old. I viewed myself through the eyes of others and all I saw was failure that I hadn't managed to breastfeed her for longer; shame at not being able to do what was 'natural'; guilt because I couldn't give my child 'the best'. In this way, I'd handed authority to others to define my worth. I was unable to be in the present moment and enjoy what I did have because I was obsessed with what I didn't have and couldn't do. And my ego regularly reminded me of all of this.

Being a 'good' mother continues to be important to me. I have not been able to let go of that attachment yet, but I am working on it. My daughters are young adults now and the challenges are different, but a lot of the struggle within me and with them results from that attachment. For example, if one of my daughters speaks to me in what could be considered an inappropriate tone or with 'rude' language, my ego feels affronted. Have I done something that might make her think her behaviour was acceptable? Am I a bad mother? I'll then direct my actions towards recovering my pride and proving my shame is unfounded in order to silence my fear, rather than stopping for a moment to consider what *she* might be feeling and why she might be speaking to me like that. Our ego immediately makes everything about us. Ironically, the other person's behaviour is rarely about us, and more likely to be about what they are going through. Maybe they are hurting? Maybe their ego has been triggered and is dictating their behaviour?

Now that I've come to know my ego more and understand how it works, I do my best to let go of what it's telling me and return to my trust in what I know to be true about myself: I try to remind myself that I am not a mother but instead I fulfil the role of a mother. This role changes as my daughters change. I am ME, and as ME I can fulfil multiple roles: mother, sister, daughter, friend, partner. But as soon as they become my identity, the ego forms an attachment, and they can turn into my prison.

In moments where I manage to remind myself of this, I realise that I can best fulfil my role as a mother when I do not allow myself to be led by emotions like pride, fear, guilt and shame, but rather let the love I feel for my daughters, the deep trust I have for myself and my fierce guide my actions.

You might recognise yourself in my story, or perhaps you have other roles that you identify with. Maybe you are attached to being a good friend? This, of course, is a wonderful thing. But when being a good friend becomes your identity, it can be restricting and prevent you from trusting yourself when things happen that fall outside of that cookie-cutter definition. Anything that might suggest that you are not a good friend will trigger you, and cause anxiety and stress. Instead, you may know that you always try your best and try to support those around you, but it is not what defines you.

When we free ourselves from the ego-driven cycle, we transform. Painful experiences offer us the opportunity to realise that we do have a choice. I can hold on to the shame and guilt that I was not a 'good mother' because I didn't have a natural birth and I didn't breastfeed as long as I wanted to. Or I can let it go, be kind to myself, know I did the best I could, and be grateful for the now.

I choose the latter. I free myself from limiting beliefs, claim my agency and decide to trust myself as I am now.

What do you choose?

Lessons learned

Trusting yourself is transforming from within.

We are enough as we are right now.

When we redefine our value system, we get to determine our worth.

When we examine the beliefs we hold about ourselves, we can let those that are limiting us go.

When we know our values, we feel confident in standing up for ourselves and reclaiming our agency.

In order to nurture trust, we need to understand our ego.

Actions

Building trust is hard. It won't happen overnight. I have highlighted a number of different actions that will help you redefine your value system, revisit your beliefs and reclaim your agency – all essential for building unconditional trust in yourself. You don't have to do them all, or do them all chronologically. Follow your instinct and do the ones that speak to you the most.

Remember, you get to decide what works for you. Trust yourself!

1. Redefine your value system

    - What questions do you hold in your mind, about yourself, that you are waiting for someone else to answer? For example, am I a good writer? Am I a good daughter? Am I a good friend? Do I deserve to be happy? Do I deserve to be treated well by those around me?

- Question those questions: write them down. YOU get to answer them. Use the beliefs work to answer your questions:

Beliefs work

- **Questions**: This is an exercise that will take time. Do not rush it. Give yourself space. Use your reflection notebook. You could choose to look at one set of beliefs a day. Write one of the questions at the top of your page and start noting down whatever comes to mind. You can start with the questions you identified above and then move on to these:
  - What do I believe I need to do/be to be liked?
  - What do I believe about myself?
  - What do I believe about my health?
  - What do I believe about my body?
  - What do I believe about myself in my role as a mother/daughter/wife/sister/friend?
  - What do I believe about pride, shame, guilt, fear?
  - Find other questions that come up as you do this work. When I was struggling with someone at work, I asked myself what I believed about that person. This can be very revealing and can help you to see that you also hold limiting beliefs about others.

- **New beliefs**: You will discover beliefs that you realise don't serve you. Write that down: *I don't want to believe this any longer.* Then write down what you want to believe instead going forward.

- **Practice**: You will need to commit to these new beliefs and practise them. You could write them on a piece of paper and hang them up in a place where you see them regularly. Or you could record a voice memo to yourself that you could listen to every morning to help you reprogramme your beliefs system.

- **Tell someone else** about this change. Ask them to remind you of this commitment you have made to yourself. Or you can write a letter to yourself with these commitments.

- **Rewrite your story**: Sit down and write a story about yourself. Write about who you are. It could start by saying something like this: 'Meet Brita. Brita is kind and compassionate. She has learned that it makes her happy when she follows her fierce ... ' By writing your story about you as you are NOW, you will erase your old narrative and deepen the ownership you feel of your new one.

- **Mantra**: Accept. Breathe. Let go. Trust your fierce. Know you are enough!

2. Reclaim your agency

- **Listen to the voice in your head**: Ask yourself whether you would say these things to your best friend or a person you love. If you would not, make a commitment to practise self-compassion.

- **Make friends with your ego**: Understand your triggers. When you feel triggered, try taking a deep breath and think about where these feelings are coming from. Practise creating a distance between your emotions and your actions.

- **Understand your attachments:** What roles are you attached to? Why are you attached to them? Can you let go of the attachment and trust that you are enough just as YOU? What would help you to let go of your attachment and do things differently?

- **Speak out:** The next time someone says or does something to you that doesn't sit right, commit to speaking out. Remember, the fear you feel right now, thinking about it, is due to the conditioning of believing you are not good enough to demand respect – we are trying to change that belief. The more you guard your boundaries, the more you will trust yourself.

- **Share your values:** Proactively tell those around you about your values and how you like to act in line with them. Explain what this will mean in terms of your behaviour and why that is. In that way you are claiming agency, defining your boundaries proactively. This can be transformative in how you trust yourself and how others around you respond to you. For example, when a new colleague starts, I always take time to explain what is important to me, and how I manage and communicate.

- **Make decisions from a place of trust:** Tapping into trust is particularly important when we are forced to make decisions. Try to practise making decisions from a place of deep trust within yourself. Where you know your values, you value yourself and you know you can take decisions that are in line with your values. I like to give myself a moment to ask myself how my decision sits with my values. That often resolves any indecision.

Chapter 5

Strength

You are stronger than you think

'Fate whispers to the warrior, "You cannot withstand the storm", and the warrior whispers back, "I am the storm."'

– author unknown

Many of us are held back by the fear that we are not strong enough to cope with challenges in life. But I have a message for you: in the most testing moments, when we face adversity, we glean an insight into just how incredibly strong we are. Even better, there is nothing we need to do other than trust the strength within us.

We are scared that we're not strong enough to cope with failure, shame, being disliked, not being needed, losing our sense of control or showing our vulnerability. We try to pre-empt how we'll cope if X, Y or Z happens to us and, when we can't see how we possibly could, we recoil. On a regular basis, I have thoughts that go along these lines:

If something bad happens to someone I love, I won't be able to cope.

If I lose my job, I will never find work again and won't be able to manage financially. I won't be able to cope.

You might think that these fears are quite valid. But cast your mind back to other hard moments you've been through:

before they happened you would probably have thought you wouldn't cope, and yet you did. The point is that constantly thinking 'I can't cope' diminishes your power, makes room for fear to flourish, and will paralyse you.

This fear often makes us attached to beliefs that do not serve us. Rather than seeing that we are afraid of the pain that comes with, for example, being alone, we believe that we are just not very good on our own, and so we stay in relationships that are not good for us. Rather than seeing that we are afraid of the pain that comes with failure and shame, we make excuses about why we're not applying for an exciting job, and so close ourselves to opportunities. This fear becomes the driving engine as we quieten our fierce. Interrogating why we think we are not strong enough is an important part of the fears to fierce journey because it helps us see the fear for what it is, enabling us to better face it.

So now let's look more closely at the following different scenarios in which you might think you're not strong enough to cope and show you that, actually, you are.

You are strong enough to fail

Several years ago, a vacancy for a bigger, more global role arose at work. I wanted to apply, but I worried I wouldn't succeed. If I was rejected, how could I continue to work for the organisation, when many would know I had 'failed'? Would my team still think I was 'good' enough? This fear that I would not be strong enough to cope with 'failure' crippled me and meant I nearly didn't go for it.

When considering whether or not to apply for the position, I thought about a similar situation I'd been in many years earlier at another organisation. A senior management job I thought I could do had come up internally, but I didn't dare apply because I was scared that I wasn't qualified and therefore wouldn't get it. Fear of failure and lack of trust in my own abilities held me back.

Even though it had been my decision to bow to my fear and let the role pass me by, I was disappointed in myself. There are so many phrases I repeat to my daughters and friends when they are in similar situations: 'You have to try, because if you don't, you'll never know'; 'There is no harm in trying'; 'What's the worst that can happen?' And yet I hadn't gone for the job because I was scared I wouldn't be strong enough to bear the 'shame' of not getting it.

So when this new opportunity arose, I remembered that feeling and decided that being **disappointed in myself for not trying was worse than feeling disappointed for *not getting it***. The former CEO of Pearson, Marjorie Scardino – the first female CEO of a FTSE 100 company – once said: 'You can fail and NOT die.' I drew on her words and resolved to go for it: to give my absolute best, be true to my passion and my belief that I could do great things in the job, *and* embrace the possibility I might NOT get it.

A few days after the interview, I was at home when the phone rang. It was the chair of the interview panel and I thought my heart would explode. She started by telling me how well I had done – and I knew immediately that I hadn't got the role.

That moment. Wow, it was physical. I could feel the sense of failure starting in the pit of my stomach and spreading all over my body. My heart raced, my head ached, and I panicked: 'What am I going to do now ... now that I've *failed*? How will I ever be able to tell my family? What will people think? This is the absolute worst. I hate the interview panel, they don't appreciate me, why did I ever apply? I'm just not good enough! My daughters will now no longer respect me ... ' And on and on went the voice in my head. Shame, anger and resentment flooded my brain at lightning speed. My ego was on fire.

But STOP. Hadn't I contemplated the possibility that I might not get it when I applied? I had made a commitment to myself to believe that if I 'failed', I wouldn't die. After all, I tell everyone that you can find strength in difficult situations and I always tell my daughters that what matters is that you tried; **results do not change who you are.**

Here I was, faced with an outcome I didn't want, and I had to prove to myself that I could live the lessons I taught everyone else: that I was strong enough to feel the pain of 'failure' and 'shame'. I thought about what I believed about my capabilities and intentions the minute before the call and then asked myself one question: why would I allow the decision of the interview panel to suddenly put all of that into doubt? It didn't make sense to suddenly start basing my worth on the decision of a small group of people made after a few hours of interview. Even though my ego was desperate to feast on the shame and anger, that realisation – that I am who I am and that doesn't change because of an external decision made by other people – was far more powerful in that moment.

It's true that this is easy to say but hard to do, because it's happening so fast. Of course, my thoughts raced, of course the pain was real. I was hurt and felt rejected. The difference this time was that, although I did allow myself to really *feel* the disappointment, I also allowed myself to observe those feelings, believing that I was strong enough to do so. **By observing them, I saw that I could choose how this would define me.** The more we choose our fierce in moments of fear, the easier it is to get through challenging situations. In those moments of choice, our strength is revealed to us.

I allowed myself 15 minutes upstairs in my bedroom. I sat on my bed and breathed. I tried to relax my stomach muscles and jaw, and then I got up and looked in the mirror and spoke to myself. I told myself that I would be fine, and then I went downstairs to see my family. I told them I hadn't got the job and shared with them the whirlwind of emotions I had felt, before explaining that I had consciously decided not to fall down the rabbit hole of self-destruction. I could see in their eyes that they felt for me, but I could also tell that they had understood that this moment of 'failure' had revealed deep strength within me.

I could see that they still respected me, and that in some ways my approach had even inspired them.

Experiencing those seconds where the pain of rejection and failure were acute, and subsequently remembering that I had a choice, made me learn about the responsibility I have to myself. Only I can choose how I respond to situations, so I want to allow my response to be guided by my strong fierce. **We have the strength to choose the response that will best nurture our fierce.**

Take a moment to think about this. Have you experienced 'failure'? What was it? How did you feel? Why did you feel like this? How might you think differently about what happened now that you know you have a choice? Have you kept yourself from trying new things because of fear of failure? What is the root of that fear?

Writing this now, years later, I don't feel any shame and I do not see the fact I didn't get the job as a 'failure'. In fact, with the power of hindsight, I know it was for the better. I was able to learn and do things I would not have been able to if I had got the job.

Thinking back to past 'failures' and seeing how much I have learned from them and grown as a result helps me when I'm faced with my fear of failure. It reminds me that even though I had been scared that I would not be strong enough to get through failure, I did. It reminds me that I am stronger than I think.

You are strong enough not to be liked

Knowing that we are stronger than we think helps us to cope with people not liking us. I have always been a person who wanted to be 'liked'. In fact, I don't think I know anyone who wants otherwise. But the reality is that there will be people who will not 'like' me. I have spent most of my life feeling I couldn't cope with people disliking me – that the pain associated with that would be stronger than me.

When I started my role as executive director, one of my main tasks was to build trust and a good working relationship with my board of trustees. Some of them were totally behind me – they backed and trusted me – some did not believe I could run the organisation, and some were undecided. Sam Collins, who was mentoring me at the time, told me that this was completely normal. In fact, the 20–60–20 rule dictates that 20 per cent of the people you work with closely are your cheerleaders: they love you, believe in you, support you. Sixty per cent are undecided: they haven't made up their minds yet, possibly don't care, or need to know more. And 20 per cent are cynical detractors, or, yes, let's say it: they don't 'like' you.[16]

So what do you do?

My initial instinct had been to focus on the 20 per cent who didn't like me and convince them that I could do the job. I thought I wouldn't be able to bear the feeling that they didn't like me. But then I thought about it. How should I best use my energy? Working closely with those who already support me? Of course. Working with those who weren't convinced yet? Definitely. Both would clearly be easier and more productive than convincing those who didn't believe in me, but that meant I had to be okay with the remaining 20 per cent not liking me. Becoming obsessed with the opinions of naysayers was no way to do my job efficiently, so I had to dig deep and focus on the 60 per cent. And do you know what? I found that I was a lot stronger than I thought. I still didn't like knowing that there were people who didn't 'like' me, but I was okay with it. Truthfully, it didn't matter, because the other 80 per cent deserved my attention.

Around this time, I came across an exercise in *Rising Strong* by Brené Brown which helped me to further understand whose

---

[16] www.presentationmagazine.com/the-20–60–20-rule-from-the-front-of-the-room

opinions I should listen to. It invites you to draw a small box.[17] Inside it, you write the names of people whose views and opinions matter to you in such a way that you would seriously consider altering the course of your actions based on what they thought. These are likely to be people you respect and love deeply. According to Brown, there shouldn't be many names in the square. My box contains six names, a mixture of family, friends and colleagues. When I worry about what other people think – especially my naysayers – I remind myself that not a single one of them is in my box.

Why don't you give this exercise a go now? Draw a box and write down the names of your top humans! This will help you to really focus on who and what matters to you. Sometimes, you'll find that by focusing on those people and yourself, your success will speak for itself and your detractors will change their minds on their own.

Learning to be satisfied with that which you cannot change is an important lesson in becoming comfortable with discomfort. It might not feel particularly nice at first, but you can bear it. Consider where you are expending energy on trying to change things or people because you fear their disapproval. What if you knew you were stronger than you thought, that you could live with people not approving of you? What would you use your energy for instead? Now that's an exciting thought!

You are strong enough not to be needed

Another fear related to our strength is the fear that we are not strong enough to cope with not being needed. As my daughters have been growing up and becoming more independent, moving schools and going to university, the way they needed me shifted. At the beginning that was hard for me. I felt silly

---

[17] Brené Brown, *Rising Strong* (Vermilion, 2015)

because they were both happy, but in reality I felt lost, lonely and a little bit heartbroken.

I was suffering because of the loss, yes, but also because I felt I was no longer needed in the same way. I had become so attached to being needed as their mother that when that identity was in flux, I felt scared. There were moments when I thought I wouldn't be able to cope. I had to learn to let go of my attachment and realise that I *am* strong enough not to be needed. My life can have meaning without being needed – on a day-to-day level at least – as a mother because, as I mentioned in the previous chapter, motherhood is a role; not the sole definition of my worth. The fear that we're not strong enough without those roles can sometimes drive us to behave in ways that don't serve us – or those around us.

Do you feel this way about parenthood? Or maybe because a friend or colleague has moved on and does not need you in the same way? Take a moment to reflect on where you have experienced this attachment of being needed. Can you notice the shift, when you understand why you felt such fear in those circumstances, because you thought you had to be needed in that specific role for your life to have a purpose?

You are strong enough not to be in control

When we feel in control of our daily lives, we feel safe from the uncertainty of instability, which we might think we are not strong enough to bear. I am sure you, like me, know people whose need to control is so overpowering that it is no longer enjoyable being in their presence. Everything is pinned down in lists, plans, details ... constant action, constant checking, constant reminders. People who are obsessively controlling seem as if they never relax. But being in control all the time is exhausting. The fear is that by letting go of control, feelings that we cannot cope with will emerge.

I had to work really hard on letting go of control and it still doesn't come easy. I notice it at work and at home. I much prefer being the person who makes decisions and puts plans in place as I see fit. That way I feel I can control the outcome of a situation, and reduce its fear factor. Holidays are a perfect example. I love planning holidays far in advance. If it was up to me, I would meticulously plan the journey, the accommodation and what we'll do on each day. That in itself might not sound so bad, but the irony is that, in my efforts to make sure everyone enjoys themselves, I become super-stressed and that affects my family too. Really, it's a lose-lose situation, where my desire to control means that I close myself off to spontaneous interactions, and other people's ideas and voices.

It's hard, but it is possible to practise letting go of control. How? The best technique I've discovered is by being present. Let me share an example with you. I plan my day by the minute: I take a certain train every morning that I cannot miss, and that determines the time I get up to go for my run, how long I have to clean the dogs and how long I spend getting ready. Because many of us need to get to work for a certain time, some of this is inevitable. When I return home in the evening, there is less pressure, so I should be able to relax, but because I have been driving myself as a minute-by-minute operation all day, I remain in that mindset. So, when Jose Luis asks me if I'd like to cook my favourite pasta with tomato sauce with him or watch our favourite Netflix series together, I instinctively say no, because it's not what I'd anticipated doing – it's not in my 'plan'. Most of the time, I don't even stop to think, 'Hold on, would I like to do this?' because I'm operating on autopilot. Now, I try to stop and remind myself of what really matters, that nothing 'bad' will happen if I let go of control, say 'Yes' to Jose Luis, and revel in this unexpected moment of joy.

If you are reading this and nodding, here's what you can do to try to switch off. Perhaps next time when you go away for a weekend, leave one of the days wide open, unplanned, to make space for spontaneity. Or perhaps you can make a commitment for a week to say yes to everything that your family members, partners or friends suggest. Make space in your life to surrender to small moments. Doing so with things like spontaneously cooking with your partner will help you practise letting go of control in bigger moments, like becoming a parent, or losing a loved one. Some things are outside of our control, and we will help ourselves if we learn that by surrendering rather than always automatically going into fight mode we actually reveal our true strength.

We realise that our fear that we are not strong enough to relinquish control is unfounded as we learn that nothing 'bad' happens when we let go. In fact, we are often rewarded with unexpected moments of joy.

Those we love are also stronger than we think

Unsurprisingly, if we fear that WE are not strong enough to cope, then we will of course also fear that those we love are not strong enough to cope.

When one of my daughters was younger, she was being bullied at school. She would come home in the evenings and tell me about the horrible things her bully, another girl, had said to her and how she had been excluded from activities during breaktime. She would often cry in bed. I would sit with her and stroke her hair while gabbling a waterfall of advice: I would speak with her teacher ... I would talk to the other girl's parents ... she should try not to let herself be affected by this ... and ... and ...

On one such evening, as I took a breath, she looked up at me and smiled: 'Don't worry, Mummy, it's okay,' she said. Her words brought me to a halt. Why was *she* comforting *me*? I realised something that she had already understood: I was scared, and everything I was saying was more about me and my fear, and less about her and how she was feeling. I looked at her and said: 'I'm not really helping you, am I?' She smiled back and said: 'No, Mummy, but that's okay.' In my desperation to protect her, I was transferring my fear that she wouldn't be strong enough to cope on to her. Her reaction allowed me to see that I had underestimated her strength.

I have the same fear when I have to give critical feedback to those I manage. I worry that they will not be able to cope with what I say, so I often try to find ways to sugar-coat it. But if I believed that my team was strong enough to take feedback, I wouldn't need to be so fearful – and they would probably benefit from my ability to be more honest.

Before you continue reading, spend a moment thinking about how you treat those you love and care for. Are you worried that they will not be strong enough? What would it look like if you stopped overprotecting and started to treat them like you knew they were strong enough? What would that look like? Can you see that it would open up a window where you support the other to believe in their strength? Where you reduce the fear not just in yourself, but in the other person? In that way, you'll nurture not just your fierce, but theirs too.

Lean into your pain

At the heart of the fear that we are not strong enough to cope with failure, or not being liked, or not being needed, or not being in control, is the fear that the pain that comes with these feelings is too much to bear. Leaning into pain, though it sounds scary – self-destructive, even – is one of the most powerful ways to uncover your strength. In fact, I have learned that I can't feel my strength without also feeling pain.

Understanding what we do to numb the pain, or hide from it, or run away from it, is the first step that will allow us to lean into the pain. In other chapters, I have spoken about the many ways that fear of pain can impact on our beliefs and behaviour patterns. Reading Brené Brown's *Rising Strong* was my 'aha' moment. She says:

> *We [numb pain] with whatever provides the quickest relief. We can take the edge off emotional pain with a whole bunch of stuff, including alcohol, drugs, food, sex, relationships, money, work, caretaking, gambling, affairs, religion, chaos, shopping, planning, perfectionism, constant change, and the Internet.*[18]

In my copy of Brown's book I underlined alcohol and perfectionism – on paper the truth became stark: my biggest emotional painkiller was alcohol.

When I was a young teenager, my parents drank regularly and allowed me to drink. Every weekend, I'd go out drinking with my friends and then went to university and did more of the same. As I started my professional life, I began drinking more at home. And then I had children, and a busy job, and my reward was a glass or two or maybe a bottle of wine in the evening. You might see yourself in my words. To me, alcohol was a fun social activity, but as I became more aware of myself, I realised I often drank to forget, as a release.

Whether it's a difficult situation in the present or a painful memory from the past that continues to inform your daily experiences, thoughts and beliefs about yourself, we put our pain-numbing methods between ourselves and those feelings. We find remedies to numb pain because we think we aren't strong enough to feel it; we fear the pain will kill us, when, really, it's often the remedies we choose that present more danger. Ultimately, they serve to dull our connection with our power.

When I read *Rising Strong*, it became crystal clear to me that I was numbing my pain and trying to ignore it. I realised, too, that I was also numbing all my other feelings. That was the killer fact:

[18] Brené Brown, *Rising Strong* (Vermilion, 2015)

you cannot selectively numb feelings – you dim all other feelings too. I did not want that. If anything, didn't I want to feel more joy, more love, more peace? Yes. I also knew that numbing the pain did not sit well with my purpose. If I wanted to inspire those around me, I had to be honest with myself and face my pain.

And so, five years ago, I gave up alcohol. Was I worried that I wouldn't be strong enough to stop? Yes. Because it is hard to stop pain-numbing habits, particularly when it seems everyone else enjoys them too. Not drinking is hard: you become the odd one out, the spoilsport, the boring one.

When you start to strip your life of those things you've used to numb pain, there will be resistance not just within yourself, but also from your surroundings. After I gave up drinking, friends stopped inviting me round in the evening, for example. But there were a few things I did that helped me to overcome my fear that I would not be strong enough to stop drinking. Firstly, I didn't tell anyone I was quitting for good. I just stopped. When people asked, I said I was taking a break. Secondly, I took it one day at a time. Very soon those days became months and, now, years. And, lastly, I remembered how I felt the morning after drinking alcohol: low energy, low mood, and disconnected from my purpose. Recalling that feeling reminded me why I was stopping, that I was practising an active choice. I believe this practice is at the heart of *in-powering* ourselves: **we have the strength to make good personal choices**. I decided that the temporary bliss of alcohol was outweighed by the depressive dimness afterwards, which erased all temptation. Since giving up, I am more present with pain and joy, and have more energy to focus on my purpose in life. **As I leaned into my pain, I discovered my strength**.

Every time I allow myself to sit with pain and discomfort, I emerge knowing that I am stronger than I think and this is something you can practise too. Spend a moment now thinking about what you do to numb, or run away and hide from your pain. What is the first thing that comes to your mind? What is a first small step you could take to stop numbing, or running and hiding from that pain? Set the intention that, at the next opportunity, you will resist the urge to numb the pain and instead you will allow yourself to feel it. To sit with it. Maybe write about it in your reflection journal. Repeat the sentence: 'I am stronger than I think.'

As you do this, remember to be kind to yourself and acknowledge the pain – because if you feel it, you can learn from it. Ignoring it or pretending it isn't there doesn't work. Telling yourself that what you are feeling is silly doesn't work either. **Take yourself seriously.** We judge ourselves so often by saying we should pull ourselves together because we think it's the brave and strong thing to do. Actually, the opposite is true: allowing yourself to feel the pain is brave and strong. I don't have to be perfect and I don't have to pretend. I can say, 'I am finding this hard.' I can be open about my vulnerability.

Angelique's story

The story I am about to tell you is an extreme example of human resilience; our ability to be strong enough to withstand pain. I want to share it with you because Angelique has inspired me so deeply with her strength and her immense vulnerability. I met her many years ago on one of my trips to the Democratic Republic of the Congo, when I first arrived at the Women for Women International office in Bukavu. Women always come and greet visitors with a song and a dance, and visitors are then encouraged to join in. As I was dancing, one woman, wearing a bright yellow blouse and skirt, caught my attention.

There was something special about her. She was tall, slim, probably a little bit older than me, and in her face I could see that she had endured experiences that had marked her profoundly. And yet there she was, in the centre of the group, dancing. I was drawn to her and I asked whether I could speak to her afterwards to get to know her. Angelique agreed and so we sat together.

I asked her about her experience of going through the Women for Women International programme. She told me what she had learned and what it had meant to her to meet other women and be part of a group, to feel a sense of belonging. Then she stopped for a moment and her body language changed. Her face became still and she told me the story of what had come before.

The militia captured Angelique during the conflict. Her husband had been killed and she, then heavily pregnant, was given the choice to either kill her unborn baby or be raped. In the end, they did both. She lifted up her blouse and she showed me the scar on her belly.

We sat there for a while, silently weeping. Holding hands. Letting the inhumanity wash over us and, for a moment, take away all hope. Cold, ugly despair seeped in. Then we took a breath. The image of Angelique dancing appeared like a mirage in my mind. She looked up to me and told me how grateful she was that she has friends again, a community. She knows she is not alone. She now wants to help others to break the sense of isolation, which so often holds us back from healing. Women for Women International had given her a way back to hope, inspiring her to believe that there is a future for her. She was now determined to do the same for others.

When I think about strength, I think of Angelique. The thought of experiencing the trauma she did and finding the strength to turn that adversity into a fire that inspires others and is a voice for change is almost unbelievable. How can you survive such pain? How can trauma like hers not break you? How can you experience something like this and not die? Angelique's story, like Beatrice's, will stay with me for ever. Her strength reminds me that we are so much stronger than we can ever imagine – an incredible lesson for us all.

Vulnerability is strength

By speaking and showing her pain so openly, Angelique taught me that there is no braver act than vulnerability. Truly showing ourselves, laying bare our very being, not hiding or numbing ourselves – those things are all examples of vulnerability, and all a sign of strength.

The #MeToo movement is inspiring to me because every woman who shared a story and opened herself up to the world made herself deeply vulnerable. It does not matter where you were born – the bravery it takes to share your story is the same; the consequences will vary in severity depending on who and where you are, but the fear you feel before you do it is the same.

Vulnerability inspires strength – when we open ourselves up, we invite others to do the same and connect in ways that are not possible if we are caged by fear.

Vulnerability often surfaces in moments of change because they're the times where we're most likely to feel unsettled and unable to cope. We can fight change or embrace it, knowing that we are stronger than we think and that with time we will get used to it, just like we have done so many times before. That memory really helps. I actively practised remembering that when I was feeling so much pain because my daughters were growing up so fast. I actively remembered that if I stay with the pain, acknowledge it and breathe and sit with it, not trying to make it go away, then eventually it will change, and become less painful. This is where what I have learned about my strength is so important, because I needed to remember that I can bear pain, even when I think I can't.

When difficult things happen to us, we have a choice. **It's not the result that defines you, but how you respond.** You can listen to your fears or listen to your fierce and trust yourself that nothing about your essence has changed.

In that way, **we can find strength in pain**. We discover our fierce in a different way. We realise there are things that happen to us which might change our circumstances or our habits, but they will not fundamentally change our fierce – in fact, they allow us to get closer to it and recognise our strength. And every time we derive strength from pain, choosing fierce over fears becomes easier.

Lessons learned

The fear that we might not be strong enough is holding us back.

You can fail and not die.

'Failure' shows us that we are stronger than we think.

You are strong enough not to be liked, needed or in control.

Feeling pain allows us to discover our strength.

Vulnerability is strength.

Actions

1. **Reflect**: Start by sitting down with your reflection journal or a piece of paper – or if you don't want to write, you can also just think about the following questions. What resonated the most from what you just read? Was it the fear of failure? Or of not being in control? Maybe you thought about your relationship with alcohol? It is also possible that something different came to your mind. Whatever it is, hold it there and really look at it. Allow yourself to feel all the feelings associated with your thoughts. Writing them down will help you to create a little bit of distance, which in turn will allow you to understand them better. Can you see that so many of your fears have at their root the fear that you will not be strong enough?

2. **Remember**: The next step is to remember one or several times where you have overcome a difficult moment. A moment where you recall feeling that you won't be able to cope. Try to remember it in as much

detail as you can. How it evolved, how you felt, how painful it was, how hard, and the fact that you DID emerge out of it. How do you feel now, looking back on it? Can you see that you were stronger than you thought? Can you capture that feeling for yourself, so you can keep it with you, as a reminder?

3. **Redefine:** Maybe the example you just thought of could also help you realise how, with the knowledge you now have, you might experience that situation differently going forward. Can you find a way to look back on difficult moments as an opportunity to learn and grow rather than as episodes that you are ashamed or embarrassed about?

4. **Stop numbing the pain:** Choose one pattern or habit you know you are using to numb your pain. Sit down and think through how you could develop a plan to help you let go of the pain suppresser. Revisit the steps I took to stop drinking alcohol. What could you do? Be kind and patient with yourself but also be determined.

5. **Know your 20–60-20:** If, like me, you struggle with knowing that you are strong enough not to be liked, why not do the 20–60-20 exercise I described above? Identify your growth champions – who are the 20 per cent who believe in you, who support you, who cheer you on? Make them your key driving force. Who are the 60 per cent who are undecided? Make them your second most important stakeholder group. And, finally, who are the 20 per cent you know are not on board with you? Decide now not to worry about them.

6. **Your VIP humans:** You can also use Brené Brown's box, where you write down your top VIP humans

who you love and respect deeply. They are the ones whose opinions matter. Keeping this box in your mind, practise going into situations without the fear of not being liked.

7. **Trust your loved ones to be strong**: Think about the people you love. What do you do out of the fear that they may not be strong enough? How could you shift that to signal, through your actions and words, that you believe in their strength? Practise this at the next opportunity. When you feel fear rising for a person you love, take a deep breath, let it go and just be present with them.

8. **Practise feeling pain**: This is a little bit like detective work. When you feel a niggle, something that doesn't feel right, go there with your attention. Find out where it is coming from. The small niggle is often a lighthouse that shows you the way to real, deep pain. When we can uncover it, not only do we pave the way to healing, we also uncover our strength.

9. **Ask for help**: You don't have to do this journey into pain on your own. I didn't. I had mentors holding my hand. Asking for help is a supreme sign of deep strength. It is often misinterpreted as a sign of weakness, but it's actually a sign that you believe in your strength and want help to get through the pain.

10. **Add another human to your boardroom in your heart**: Let this be someone who has inspired you deeply with their strength. As you can imagine, Angelique has a seat at my boardroom table. In moments where I fear that I will not be strong enough to cope, I go to my boardroom and meet Angelique. She always reminds me that I am stronger than I think.

Chapter 6

Love

Choose love every day

'The most important thing in life is to learn how to give out love, and to let it come in ... We think we don't deserve love, we think if we let it in we'll become too soft. But a wise man named Levine said it right. He said, "Love is the only rational act."'

– Mitch Albom, *Tuesdays with Morrie*[19]

Initially, I was going to call this chapter 'Positivity'. For a long time, I thought that what helped me to be the most effective version of myself was being positive. Those around me reinforced this. People would say: 'Brita, you are just *so* positive ...' and I would embrace their praise while promoting a glass-half-full attitude.

Sometimes, though, I would hear people say that it was unrealistic to expect everything to burst with 'positivity' and I began to feel uncomfortable, because I felt I was labelling an approach to life in a way that made others seem 'negative'. That, of course, was the exact opposite of what I wanted to do. I am passionate about us all embracing our fierce as it is and finding our own way. As soon as I realised that I had caught

[19] Mitch Albom, *Tuesdays with Morrie* (Sphere, 2003)

myself unawares in the midst of yet another binary, I asked myself what I really meant when I promoted positivity. When I thought about it, I realised the answer was LOVE.

Love is such an important part of the fears to fierce journey because it has a dual purpose: nurturing unconditional love for ourselves, and acting with love towards others. These two benefits are interconnected and cyclical, because when we love ourselves unconditionally, we can extend that love to those around us *and* the wider world. At the same time, loving others helps us to nurture love for ourselves, which makes us more compassionate self-leaders. **Love inspires love**.

Rather than trying to put a positive spin on a situation, try viewing it (and yourself) with love. What do I mean by that? I don't mean romantic love, or frivolous 'I *love* chocolate' love. When I say *love,* I mean a state where we consciously, proactively, and in the present, feel deep gratitude for being here right now. Let me give you an example, because I know this might sound a little abstract.

I'll often use my morning train commute as an opportunity to practise love. I do this on purpose because being on the London Underground is *not* my favourite moment of the day, but it is a great opportunity to practise connection, an (inner!) stillness, joy and contentment. I look around myself and, as I see other passengers, I send them warm feelings. I remember how much we all struggle inside and embrace them in my thoughts as my fellow humans. Even if someone pushes me, I take a deep breath and extend feelings of understanding and compassion towards them.

Extending love in these situations is hard because it requires us to rise above what we cannot understand and extend love anyway. I recently read an article on Medium.com called 'Laziness Does Not Exist'. In it, the writer Devon Price says: 'When you don't fully understand a person's context – what it feels like to be them every day, all the small annoyances and major traumas that define their life – it's easy to impose abstract, rigid expectations on a person's behaviour ... If a person's behaviour doesn't make sense to you, it is because you are missing a part of their context.'[20] When someone does something that you find hard to understand – perhaps it seems mean or spiteful – show them love anyway and don't assume the worst: you just don't understand their motive. Feelings of warmth, compassion, connectedness, kindness and gratitude are all signs of the deep love I am talking about.

What is love?

Let's delve a little deeper into what this kind of love looks like ...

It's universal

We often think of love as something we have for another person, for our family, close friends, partners; but the love I'm talking about is a love that knows no boundaries. It does not distinguish between love for people in your private life, your professional life and those you don't know. It's universal. I know it sounds strange to think that we can feel love for everything. Of course, there are moments where we might feel it more easily because we recognise it clearly, such as the love we might have for our children. I used to think I could never love anything as much as my daughters, but the love I have for Emma and Sara has shown me how deeply I am capable of loving. You might not be able to extend loving feelings towards your fellow commuters immediately, but the transformation you're undergoing on the fears to fierce journey will pave the way to loving yourself and others more.

[20] www.humanparts.medium.com/laziness-does-not-exist

It's unconditional

When you stop and feel the love I describe, you can sense that it *is* unconditional in its very nature. This kind of love does not have any conditions attached to it. If it has, then it isn't love. To me, this is the most important, impactful aspect of the loving approach I advocate. I have told you how much I've struggled with the notion of being a 'good girl' and the fear that if I wasn't a good girl, I wouldn't be lovable ... Well, with this love I get to love myself no matter what – good girl or not! When we realise we can love ourselves unconditionally, it quietens the critical voice in our head. It allows us to be present, and to love others in turn.

It's fearless

Loving helps us to choose fierce over fears. We can still feel fear when we feel love, but we can choose to act with love rather than fear. If I unconditionally love myself, I don't have to be scared that I'm not worthy of love because my mere existence makes me deserving and I don't have to hold love back for fear of getting hurt. I have many friends who, over the years, have been scared to love. They would calculate when, how and how much they should love. If you feel love and fear at the same time, search inside yourself to understand what you are scared of and how that would change if you loved yourself unconditionally. Where is this fear coming from? What is it attached to? It's often a memory or a person who is important to us, and I'll talk about this later in the chapter. For now, trust me, this kind of love trumps fear.

It's accepting

When we love, we accept whoever it is – ourselves, or someone else – for who they are and resist judging them. Love doesn't operate in labels, but envelops and embraces all that there is. When we feel love deeply, nothing else matters. You don't make a list of all the 'good' aspects and 'bad' aspects and then decide to love the person because the 'good' outweigh the 'bad'. When you love, you love all of it. If not, you're not really 'loving' but selectively liking based on judgement.

It's unthinking

We cannot *think* about love or try to rationalise it and be present with it at the same time. Experiencing all-encompassing love requires us to feel rather than think because love simply is; it cannot be labelled and it doesn't judge. It works both ways: when we allow deep love, we're present. And by being present we allow love. Can you think of a moment when you've felt like this? I often do when I am in nature. Suddenly I am no longer thinking, I just am, and I feel at peace, with love in my heart, which isn't directed at anyone or anything.

It's infinite

There is no such thing as too much love. Loving in this way does not mean that you cannot argue, disagree or have difficult conversations – with yourself or with others. Sometimes, we think we should not love so much, because it means we're a 'walkover'. It implies that loving too much makes us weak. Sometimes, the way we speak about love implies we have a limited amount that we must carefully apportion. This deep love is all about *going for it*. Loving yourself as deeply as you possibly can, knowing that it's infinite – and so is your capacity to give it.

Love nurtures our fierce

You'll notice that the sort of love we're trying to nurture for ourselves and other people is closely connected to our fierce.

Before you continue reading, stop for a moment and really take this in: **love is the power that nurtures our fierce;** the beating heart of our fears to fierce journey.

Love helps us to be free

Nurturing love for others and ourselves helps us find freedom from attachments to feelings like anger, hate and resentment – all of which are derived from our inner pain, but which we often blame others for. How do I know this? Over the years, I've searched inside myself to try to understand the pain I feel and I've learned that I was blaming others in my life for my pain.

Many of us blame our parents for how we feel. It makes sense: our parents brought us into the world and we are attached to feeling dependent on them. It is hard to free them and ourselves from this attachment and claim responsibility for who we are, and this has definitely been the case for me. I have blamed my parents for all sorts of feelings and this blame blocked my ability to fully love myself and believe I am worthy of love.

For so long, I blamed my mother for my feelings of insecurity because I felt she had not protected me enough when she was a single mum, and those emotions caused me pain. Even knowing that releasing my mother would release me, my attachment was so strong that I didn't want to.

This is how I managed to do it.

I had been working with a coaching client who was in a similar situation to me. She was feeling a lot of anger and resentment towards her brother and mother, and had become attached to those feelings. They were holding her back from uncovering her potential and finding peace. I suggested she write a letter to them. Not to send, but because I sensed that the act of writing directly to them would help her find closure. A few days afterwards, I told the woman who was training me as a coach at the time, Moira Spence, about this. We spoke about other things and towards the end of the session we ended up talking about my mother. Moira suggested I should write a letter to her, just like I had suggested to my client. When I heard this, my body reacted almost violently. There was no way I was going to do this. I wasn't fully aware why I was reacting like this, but now I know: I *needed* to blame my mother, so I brushed off Moira's suggestion.

A few months later, I was sitting in the garden, thinking about this chapter and wondering why I didn't feel unconditional love for myself. It took me to thinking about my relationship with my mother and I realised that blaming her for my pain was the reason. And if I was serious about wanting to unconditionally love myself, I was going to have to let that go.

So I did as Moira had advised and wrote a letter to my mother in my notebook. The first sentence I wrote was: 'I release you, Mama. I know you love me and you have always loved me and you did the best you could.' It was one of my most powerful moments of transformation. The letter goes on, honest and real and full of love. Love for myself and for my mother – as another human – free from expectations, blame and guilt. And I did not send it.

This is what I call 'releasing with love' – doing this frees us and creates space for more love. When we allow ourselves to know where these feelings come from, we can release them with love and find freedom within ourselves. **The act of releasing with love is one way of exercising unconditional love for ourselves.**

Think about what feelings of anger, resentment and hate you feel attached to. Why do you think you are so attached to them? Who are they directed at? Do you sense that those feelings are stopping you from fully loving yourself? Could you write a letter to that person whereby you release them with love, both for yourself and them? You don't have to send it. Remember this is about giving *you* the inner peace that you desire. This takes time, but when you do it, you'll feel free in an almost revolutionary way.

Get out of your head and into your heart

As I've already said, we cannot *think* love, so the most important action we can take to nurture and cultivate it is to get out of our heads and into our hearts.

How? By surrendering to feeling love in as many areas of your life as you can. I have started to do this consciously, like on my commute! When I meet people, I try to become aware of how I evaluate the person in my head and the thoughts that are going through my mind. I then consciously move my attention downwards to my heart and I ask myself: what do I feel? Yes, you can *feel* a person. When you seek to understand another person through feelings rather than judgemental thoughts, you're practising love. Once you start meeting people with love, you realise how much more you are able to know about them beyond what you can see or hear. In fact, switching off my thoughts sometimes gives me the greatest insights.

Another effective way I have found of getting out of my head and into my heart is by practising gratitude. I find that appreciating where we are, what we have and how we feel right *now* brings us closer to love, closer to being. When we're present, we're not living in the past, attached to painful memories, and we are not in the future, full of expectations that we have no control over.

Try this now. Stop for a moment, look up, and think about something you are grateful for. Notice how you feel. Can you feel the love that comes with this gratitude? Practising gratitude is akin to practising unconditional love for ourselves. As we cultivate gratitude for what we have and what is around us, we change the narrative from a story where we don't have and are not enough – and are therefore unlovable – to a story where we have and are enough and are therefore lovable. There are some great exercises for practising gratitude in this chapter's action plan.

Acting with love

'We can't choose to vanish the dark, but we can choose to kindle the light.'

– Edith Eger, *The Choice* [21]

When we look around at the conflicts in the world, the violence and hate, love can sometimes be hard to see. But finding love everywhere is possible – it's about choosing to see it.

Three years ago, to coincide with International Women's Day, my team and I at Women for Women International came up with a new campaign called #MessageToMySister where we invite supporters to write a message of solidarity and hope to a woman living in a country affected by conflict. We knew what receiving messages from other people, sometimes thousands of miles away, meant to the women in the organisation's programme: that there was someone thinking of them, a simple and powerful affirmation of their existence, an act that told them: 'I see you.'

The first year we did it, I couldn't stop reading the messages that came in from across the world. They were full of love! It was as if the campaign had given permission for love to come out of hiding. These messages also showed me how much we all yearn to be loved ourselves. Because when you write a message to someone you don't know and will never meet, you write what YOU want to read. Since launching, over 5,000 messages have been written from over 80 countries – and every single one is in stark contrast with the daily news. In fact, at times it seems like a parallel universe.

[21] Edith Eger, *The Choice* (Rider, 2017)

I know which universe I choose.

In my work, I see people acting with love every day, even in the most testing and traumatic of situations. I'd like to tell you a particularly powerful story about a trip I took to Bosnia in 2015, which shows the power of acting with love …

Latif's story

It is 40 degrees and the sun is beating down, scorching the dry ground. I'm taking part in a 120km peace march across Bosnia from Tuzla to Srebrenica, where the 1995 genocide took place, to commemorate its twentieth anniversary. Over 15,000 people had fled from the Srebrenica genocide to seek shelter in the safe zone of Tuzla. The march is a symbolic reversal of the route those fleeing would have taken. Sara and Emma had wanted to come, so they joined the group of Women for Women International supporters who were accompanying us.

The beginning of the march is tense and there are police everywhere. Thousands of Bosnians have come from abroad to join. It is also the first time Emma and Sara are experiencing first-hand why I do what I do. I'm nervous. Sara is only 12 and I worry about how she will feel. It is one thing learning about history and its cruelty from school books, but quite another to see and feel what historic facts mean to people who live them. But as you'll know by now, I have learned to trust my fierce and ignore the niggling voice that tells me not to do things.

We stay overnight at the homes of graduates of the Women for Women International programme. In the evening, we share *ajvar* – a traditional Bosnian red pepper puree – and homemade cheese-filled pastries. The next morning, we set off early to join the march for the second day. I ask Latif, our guide, whether I can walk with him and talk about his experience of the war.

Latif was 16 when he had to flee over the mountains. He left Srebrenica in a group of over 2,000 and when he arrived in the safe zone of Tuzla after 78 days, he was one of 20. Some of his friends fell victim to landmines, others got ill, some were killed by soldiers. His father and two brothers didn't make it. Latif's father and one of his brothers are buried at a memorial centre and, two years ago, he buried the remains of his other brother. I struggle to imagine what it must have been like to wait 18 years to be sure that your brother has been killed; to say goodbye, to grieve. Latif tells me his mother didn't come to the funeral because she couldn't bear the pain.

As we continue talking, we pass a mass grave containing over 500 bodies. I ask Latif how he thinks the country can move forward from this horror. He is clear: despite 100 war criminals being sentenced, justice has not been done. He says many of his friends and their families know who killed their relatives and see those people going about their everyday lives, with impunity. He looks at me: what would you do, Brita? That, of course, is the question I've been silently asking myself all along.

After my conversation with Latif, I walk alone for a long time, putting one foot in front of the other and thinking. I can see how important it is to have justice, an acknowledgement of wrongdoing. Sweeping it under the carpet and hoping it will go away does more harm and will never enable Bosnians to move on. Wherever we go, there is a story of how the genocide has affected people. Real stories. Real pain. Real horror. The darkness of what humanity is capable of feels unfathomable. How could Latif feel anything other than pain?

On the last day, I see another way. Ten kilometres from Srebrenica, the group weary and down, we stop for a rest at the side of the road. As we sit under the shade of a tree, a man comes and gives us cold cartons of juice and plastic cups. The juice tastes like nectar. I'm filled with gratitude and so humbled by this man's kindness that I want to thank him again. He tells me that in this tiny village, over 120 people were killed during the genocide, including his sons and his wife. He also showed me his foot, which had been sliced in half and sown back together by the very people who had killed his family. I struggle to keep my composure. He goes on to tell us how grateful he is that we are doing the peace march, because it is important to him that the world does not forget, that the death of his family should not be in vain.

We say goodbye. As we continue walking, the tears I have been fighting back start flowing. I am overwhelmed by the man's grief for his wife and his sons, but I am profoundly, life-changingly, moved by the small act of love he showed us. Moments like these reveal in one split second the worst and the best of humanity. Just when you think the pain of what you are hearing might be too much, you see a ray of light. When you follow it, you see that this ray of light has **love** at its source. How this man found his way out of pain and fear to love, I don't know. But now he can fulfil his purpose: ensuring the world doesn't forget the horrors of Srebrenica.

I have seen many people emerge from pain with profound love in their hearts. I know that **love is a powerful force which can conquer all pain and fear.** Love is within us all, for us to tap into when we need to heal. And, as we heal, we connect more deeply to our fierce.

When Latif asked me what I would do if faced with the injustice of knowing that the perpetrators of genocide and killers of my family were living free, I didn't know what to say. But after hearing the story of the man who gave us juice, I began to formulate an answer. I believe it is the right of anyone who has experienced a crime to see justice done, but I also know that justice does not bring freedom. **The peace you yearn for after something horrific has happened is a peace that can only come from within you.**

If I were to meet Latif again, I'd tell him that I would search deep within myself for the infinite love that resides in each one of us, and try to release my feelings of hate and anger, so that I may find inner peace. I don't know if I would manage it, because I have never been in Latif's situation, but I would hope for it – and love would be at the core of that hope. In my work I have seen women and men who have experienced trauma like

Latif's and that of the man who gave me his juice and, for many, love has helped them find a path to peace.

Choose love

If you allow yourself to live in pain by holding on to rage, resentment or hate, you'll slowly erode from the inside and feel constantly disconnected from your fierce. Of course, I don't want to label anger as a 'negative' emotion – it can be a brilliant fuel for driving social change. But there will always be a time you'll need to release your anger, its purpose served, for your inner wellbeing. I know this from my own experience. Do I feel angry at the injustice in the world? Absolutely YES! Has it propelled me forward? Absolutely YES. But when I needed to heal, it wasn't anger that helped, but love. The process of recovery is sometimes referred to as forgiving or forgetting, but it's neither of those things: it's about releasing the pain with love for yourself.

Love allows me to recover from the sadness and despair I feel when I hear the stories of people like the man who gave us juice in Bosnia. What inspired me more than anything was the love he showed us despite (or maybe because of) the pain of his experience. That love nurtures my fierce because it reminds me that there is always a way to freedom even from the deepest pain. Knowing that gives me the courage and the ability to focus on the *why*. Why are we here? What is our purpose? In this way, receiving love helps me to stay centred on my purpose, and to follow my purpose with love, too.

For some, the concept of love feels incongruous with certain parts of our lives – work, for example. I have read many management books and few talk about the importance of love. In fact, many speak about keeping our work and personal lives separate and warn against becoming too close to colleagues. I know it is unconventional to speak about love at work and to cultivate love in a work team, but that's exactly what I do.

Because love allows us to connect, find freedom and therefore uncover our potential, it made so much sense to me to bring it to work. After all, did I not want to work in a highly motivated team who uncovered their potential and changed other people's lives in turn?

I set about purposefully introducing love into our ways of working and our values. Together as a team we defined how we wanted to interact with each other. The loving kindness that our team is committed to has transformed the way we all work. It propels us to be flexible and supportive of each other's life circumstances, and when we treat each other with love, we enable each other to fulfil our purposes.

Choosing to turn up with love creates a sense of ease and a space where people can 'in-power' themselves and reach for more ambitious goals. I know that the love my team and I have for our communal purpose and colleagues is a huge motivating factor for all of us. Love creates possibilities and encourages us to find compassionate ideas and solutions that foster love further. I always sign all my emails with 'Love'; it is a simple way of reminding myself how I want to be in the world.

And when it comes to the tough stuff? I have criticised with love and let people go with love. Just because someone isn't right for the job any more does not mean I don't still love and appreciate them. You can even be angry with love. I have been angry with a family member and felt the deep love I have for them at the same time. Remember, this is not about love or hate, compassion or anger, but combining the seemingly un-combinable, because the reality is that we all have these conflicting emotions within us.

Of course, it's sometimes hard to choose love when we encounter those who are not open to it. Their reactions might trigger our ego and we might make assumptions about that person. But know this: we can meet rejection with love too. If we can understand the root of the rejection to be their pain, we can empathise, because we know our own pain.

Approaching my family, colleagues and the women who Women for Women International serves with love is the single most meaningful thing I do. And it's cyclical: love creates inner peace and peace among those with whom we interact, because you cannot fight against love.

Cultivating unconditional love for yourself and acting with it when you're out in the world is, ultimately, what brings peace to nations. Love is the most life-changing force any of us have at our disposal and is therefore a vital part of the fears to fierce journey.

Lessons learned

Love is a powerful force and can conquer fear and pain.

Love is fearless, non-judgemental, present, universal and infinite.

Love is the beating heart of our fears to fierce journey and nurtures our fierce.

Love allows us to release our attachment to anger, resentment and hate.

The love you give to yourself is the love you give to others and vice versa.

You can choose love, even in the most unlikely situations.

Actions

Practise love

The only way you will cultivate love for yourself and others is with practice. I do many of the actions I've listed below several times a day. I hope they inspire you and might spark other ideas. Above all, I hope you will see that choosing love is not a weird, far-out, wishy-washy notion, but a practical and concrete way to nurture your fierce.

- **Make a gratitude list**: When I lie in bed in the evening, I always think of three things that I am grateful for that have happened that day. When I began doing this, I noticed a shift within myself: rather than focusing on what hadn't gone well and judging myself, I reset my thinking and started to show myself love instead. As soon as I lie in bed, I get excited to think of the things I'm grateful for. This practice has exponentially increased my love for myself. Others write them down – which you can do of course. Make it work for you.

- **Spread love through appreciation**

  - Take a moment – right now – to **send a message** to someone you appreciate. Tell them you're thinking of them and that you love them. Imagine how great it would feel to be on the receiving end of a message like that? When I first started telling people who weren't my family or close friends that I loved them, it felt a little strange, but the more you do it, the more comfortable you'll feel. It helps you to realise the infinite capacity for love that we all have.

  - Every so often, I end staff meetings with an **'appreciation round'**. I start by telling the person next to me what I appreciate about them, and they then appreciate the person sitting next to them, and so on until it comes full circle. It is my favourite thing to do. Not only do I learn something new every time, but I am also deeply moved by the love and kindness that is so clearly present among my team. Try this with your family, a group of friends, or at work!

  - At a recent staff party, everyone contributed to a **bag filled with love** – everyone chose a small thing they love and bought one for every colleague. Each person received a bag filled with 36 special things that their colleagues love. They ranged from exotic tea bags, to special sweets, poems and recipes. The previous year we prepared appreciation bags, where everyone had written a note of appreciation for each colleague, resulting in a bag with 36 appreciative notes for each one of us. You might have other ideas; try them out at work or with friends.

- **Practise loving thoughts:** You can do this for anyone or anything. Think of someone and feel the love you have for that person, but don't tell them about it. Just allow yourself to feel the love and nurture loving thoughts. I always sign off on my messages with: 'Love', or 'Gratitude'. It reminds me that this is the state I want to be in! Try doing it in a situation you normally wouldn't – it might feel weird at first but your interaction will be filled with a kindness that wasn't there before.

- **Release with love:** Think about what feelings of anger, resentment, hate you feel attached to. Why do you think you are so attached to them? Who are they directed at? Could you write a letter to that person where you release them with love for yourself and for them, just like I did with my mother? You don't have to send it. Remember, this is about you! But just writing it all down will free you in wonderful ways.

- **Meet people with love:** Consciously practise meeting people with love. You can follow the steps I outlined earlier when I spoke about getting out of your head and into your heart. When I do this, I pay attention to the usual judgements I would make about the person and the impending interaction, and I let them go as I focus on loving myself and the other person – without conditions. Try this: when you meet a close family member, focus on love when you interact with them. The more you do this, the easier it will be to feel love on a more regular basis, and soon you'll be able to extend the practice to everyone you encounter.

- **Shower yourself with love:** Apply the way you practised sending loving thoughts, warmth and compassion to others to yourself. Close your eyes and imagine warm sunlight enveloping your body, feel the warmth on your skin and inside your body. Feel the love you have so easily for others in your heart and direct it towards yourself. Send yourself loving thoughts. Embrace yourself in your mind.

- **Help each other to find a way back to love:** We all get stressed and there are times when we don't feel the love. Loving ourselves is an ongoing commitment and it is one we can help each other to keep. In 2019 I promoted Women for Women International's then director of fundraising and communications, Shivonne Graham, to co-director of Women for Women International because the organisation's development needed it and I wanted to have a co-leader. It might be seen as an unusual model of leadership, but it works because we can support each other to play to our strengths and deliver the best for the organisation. When I see that Shivonne is getting stressed, for example, I find a time where we sit together and I support her in stopping for a moment, remembering our purpose, and approaching every situation with love. And she does the same for me.

Fear keeps us from turning up with love, and together we can identify the fear and find a way through it that makes space for love again. Knowing we are not on our own is a key part of enabling us to commit to love. Who can you ask to help you in moments where you need someone to remind you of your commitment to choosing love? Now go and ask this person to be there for you when you need them to remind you of your commitment to practising love. In times where you find it hard to nurture love, call them or meet with them.

Chapter 7

Care

Be your own life vest

'Self-care is often building strong foundations so that we can weather the life-storms.'

– Jayne Hardy

I was 29 when my first daughter was born. Emma was a much-loved baby from the very first moment. I could not have been more excited and being a mother was hugely important to me. I had tried not to read many baby books because I worried they might make me feel inadequate and overwhelmed. Instead, I preferred to trust my own instincts. But even without reading those books, I had my own set of expectations as to what being a 'good mother' would entail. One of them was to always prioritise my children. It wasn't difficult, because I had never felt such love and it consumed me (and I know this feeling can be the same with other relationships). But what I know now that I didn't know then is that **you don't have to sacrifice yourself for your children – or anyone else.**

I went back to work eight months after having Emma and nine months after I gave birth to Sara. I had to for financial reasons, but I also really wanted to. Staying at home was not bringing out the best in me. I loved my work and was happy to be back, but everything had changed. Being torn became the norm. And feeling guilty became part of my everyday experience.

Part of the way in which I coped with the guilt I felt about being a working parent was to ensure that every single minute of my remaining time was dedicated to my children. The price I had to pay for going to work, I believed, was me. By de-prioritising myself, I would feel less guilty. Feeling no guilt at all was out of the question; my new mission was about moderating how much guilt I felt.

Gone were the days when I would idly leave work around six o'clock, sometimes half past or seven o'clock, or chat for an hour at team lunches. Suddenly, time took on a different dimension. It was measured by the time with my children and the time I was *not* with my children. Time not with my children had to be maximised in order to justify being away from them. My working hours were strict: I started at eight o'clock so that I could leave at four o'clock to pick up the girls from nursery and, later, school. I packed everything into the eight hours I had. I no longer took lunch breaks and became far less sociable. And when the second hand on the clock ticked past four, I was like a woman possessed in my mission to get to the girls.

I worked out that the fastest way to get from work to nursery was by scooter, so I would race through London, narrowly avoiding accidents at every corner. Once back at our flat, I would prepare and feed them dinner, bathe them, before reading them a story and putting them to bed. I would often fall asleep singing lullabies and then get up again the next morning at six o'clock to go to work, leaving before the girls rose. Jose Luis took the morning shift and would get them up, make breakfast and take them to nursery.

Weekends were precious. They were the only time we spent all together. I would go for a morning run on Saturdays and Sundays – and that was my me-time. Other than those brief jogs, it didn't even occur to me to do something that was just about me. As the girls grew older, I advanced in my 'career', and my responsibilities at work increased. My passion for my children and my work were my drivers – and I drove myself fast. Then, gradually, the signs appeared. As soon as work stopped for Christmas at the end of the year, I would be bedridden with a bad flu bug. It was like clockwork. Then, my dentist pointed out my even bite – it turned out I'd been systematically grinding my teeth in my sleep without even noticing – and soon it started giving me headaches. Clearly, my body was saying: Enough! But I didn't listen.

I began speaking to Moira, my coach. She contacted Women for Women International because she wanted to help women working for other women and has supported and mentored me over the years. Moira has a seat in the boardroom in my heart, for all the wisdom and love she has given me. She reminded me of the advice you're given on airplanes about **putting your own life vest on before helping anyone else** – even your children. When she said it, I remembered that I'd always thought the suggestion was crazy: I simply could not envisage trying to save myself before my children. Intellectually, I understood the logic that if you're not there, you can't save anyone, but, emotionally, I couldn't do it.

Eventually, through the annual flu, the teeth-grinding and the conversations with Moira, I came to see the importance of taking care of myself. Would doing so mean that I wasn't a good mother? Of course not. The stories that I had created and believed about how I should divide my time in order to be the perfect parent were fallacies and, ironically, by paying more attention to my own needs, I might actually be a more present, less exhausted mother.

From my own experience and working with many women over the years, I know that **looking after ourselves, putting ourselves first, is not something that comes naturally.** You might feel like this too. It is directly linked to how much we believe that we matter and to how we define our worth. This goes back to what I spoke about in chapter 4: if we believe we are not good enough, we won't find it easy to stop and look after ourselves because we don't believe we're worthy of such care. That's why this chapter is devoted to helping you to see your own worth and care for yourself.

If you are the change, you need to care for yourself

Taking care of yourself is intrinsically linked to the personal transformation you are seeking by reading this book. In fact, the aphorism 'Be the change you want to see' is key. If *you* are the change, *you* are the most important thing, and therefore **taking care of yourself is an investment in your most precious asset.**

There are two important realisations that have helped me to commit to caring for myself. Firstly, I realised that no one else is going to do it for me. We so often wait for others to take care of us. People can help us, but we need to take responsibility. It all links back to agency, to being in charge of your life. Caring for yourself is saying: 'I matter.'

Secondly, I realised that I was often making the excuse that I didn't have time. Do you do this? What does taking time out mean to you? To me, it's removing myself from the grind of daily obligations, extricating myself from the pressure to be 'productive' in all areas of my life.

You might have forgotten this amid life's burdens, but *you* are in charge of *your* time – nobody else. So why do we give responsibility for how we spend it to others, rather than claiming it for ourselves? We say, 'I don't have time,' blaming work, our children, our partners, life, but if I don't allow myself time, that's my choice; I cannot blame anyone else for it.

Boundaries

One of the most important aspects of caring for yourself is defining and owning your boundaries. Only you can decide what is good for you and what is not. In some cases, caring for ourselves will mean enduring a relationship even if it isn't fulfilling what we need because it's too hard to break the bond. Everyone's reality is different, and what constitutes looking after yourself for one person might be entirely different for another, and it can also change.

Your boundaries are yours, and yours alone. A friend of mine has a difficult relationship with her mother. She doesn't make her feel good and says horrible things to her. Even though this friend has committed to loving and respecting herself, she knows that every time she visits her mum, her boundaries might falter. Looking after herself while also caring for her mum with love and compassion seems like a near-impossible task, but it is more important to her to maintain a careful balance than it is to protect herself by not going.

We get to define what works for us. We draw our boundaries and we shift them when we want. But because we do not exist in a vacuum, we need to communicate our boundaries and protect them. Expressing what we need sounds simple, but it is hard because we often don't know what we need. When we don't know what is good for us or how to care for ourselves, how are we supposed to explain it to those around us? Caring for ourselves is powerful because it enables us to get to know ourselves so that we may then share that knowledge with those around us.

I know that I don't often ask for what I need. Many of us don't. Why? Because we believe there's a stigma attached to it. If we say what we need, we worry that we'll be perceived as 'selfish'. It goes back to the belief that we should be selfless in order to fulfil the expectations of what makes a good woman, wife, mother, daughter, friend – or fill in the blank!

But no more! We know now that we need to put ourselves first by finding out what works for us, what we need, and then ensuring that we make time for it. As you carve out time to care for yourself and define your own boundaries with love, it'll be transformational and empowering, and you will inspire those around you to do the same.

Body, mind, heart, fierce

All of the practices in the care toolkit below have one thing in common: they are holistic, in that they benefit my body, mind, heart *and* fierce. Be aware of how your care practice impacts on these different aspects of yourself. I know, for example, that the meditation you're about to read quietens my mind, which has made me far more focused and concentrated when it comes to my work commitments. It also helps my body, because I relax my jaw and shoulders and feel physically much better. In that moment of pause, I nurture gratitude and feel love for the people around me, filling my heart. This feeling then inspires me and connects me to my fierce. When I run every morning, I look after my body, I organise my mind (I always go through any worries in my head and by the time I am back home I know what I'm going to do!), and the gratitude I feel for my dogs and the beautiful countryside connects me to my heart and my fierce. In this way, all of my care practices nurture all aspects of me, my whole being.

My care toolkit

Over the years, I have developed my own toolkit of things that help me to look after myself, which I reveal below. I didn't sit down one day and say, 'From now on I need to look after myself,' then write this list. I developed it over years and it works for me. I still add new things when I come across something I love, and I also take things off the list that no longer work for me. We change and our needs change, so stay in touch with what works for you.

The below are the principles and practices in my care toolkit. I've listed them so that you might feel inspired. Take the ones that chime with you and integrate them into your own life, but, as you read, think about other things that you would like to do. In this way, you'll start to build your own personal toolkit.

A note on care: **one of the biggest risks with committing to it is that we use it as a stick to beat ourselves with.** It's so ironic. Every time I find myself scolding myself in my head because I haven't meditated or relaxed enough, I laugh ... then stop, notice it and realise that maybe, in that moment, all the care that I can manage is NOT being harsh on myself. And that is okay! Your care commitments aren't a straitjacket.

You might have noticed that I've called this chapter and this toolkit 'Care', as opposed to 'Self-care'. The latter has become such an overused term that, at times, it feels like a throwaway phrase without much meaning. In fact, truly caring for yourself is such an important notion that I want you to consider the concept afresh as simply 'care' and really engage with it.

Meditation

Be more, do less

Meditation is something I started doing six years ago and it has been my most transformational care practice.

Before, when others suggested I try meditating, I worried that I didn't have time, I wouldn't be 'good' at it, it 'wasn't for me', I didn't know how. You might have other reasons, but those were mine, and I think they are quite common.

In 2012, brand new in my role as executive director and needing help, I began working with Sam Collins, who had agreed to mentor me for six months. She taught me a key lesson: **be more, do less.** In order to live this philosophy, she suggested I give meditation a go, but it wasn't until three years later that I was able to wrap my head around it, and work out how to integrate it into my life.

When, in 2014, someone told me about Headspace, a meditation app, I was ready – the time had finally come to commit.

Downloading the app with a single tap on my phone made it almost irresistibly simple. Headspace allows users to meditate for however long they choose and it took away some of my fear. I decided to use my train journeys to work to meditate for ten minutes every morning. I had to find a regular time slot, otherwise I was going to find it hard to commit to a new practice. The commute worked for me. I don't meditate daily, but now I have at least a few moments every day where I stop, focus on my breath and tune in to my body.

You can do this now. Close your eyes, put your hands on your tummy and take a deep breath. Really feel how the air fills your lungs and notice how, as you breathe out, you let go of tension. For the next breath, notice where you are holding tension in the body. You don't have to do anything about it. Just acknowledging it is enough.

This practice alone has been revolutionary for me. Not that long ago, I was preparing for a very stressful meeting, which I knew was going to make me feel defensive, fearful, angry ... basically, the emotions that can easily become overwhelming in moments where you want to keep calm. I used the breathing and noticed where in my body I could feel these emotions during the meeting. Perceiving the knot in my stomach, the anger in my chest, enabled me to feel the stress and breathe through it – it was as if, by noticing the tensions in my body, I could allow them to flow through, rather than overpower, me. By noticing, we create a distance of just a fraction of a second. This time gives us a choice: to follow that feeling of anger and express it, or let it go.

Don't get me wrong – I often choose to express my anger and give in to my ego, but the times where I don't are precious and make me appreciate my meditative practice. These are the moments when I know I am following my purpose, creating the impact I want around me.

When I first started regularly tuning in to my body, I realised I would tense my stomach muscles, clench my teeth and hold my breath almost constantly. There was so much tension in my body and, until then, I'd had no idea. It was as if I was living in a state of fear, and I felt the need to be always ready for an attack. Once I realised what was happening, I was gradually able to let it go. Every time I focused on my breath, I checked in with my abdominals and released them. When I did, something shifted within me physically, but I was also able to adjust my approach to decision-making – moving from reactive to reflective. I changed how I responded to difficult situations by embracing them as opportunities to learn.

If you find yourself getting stuck on the word 'meditation', you don't have to call it that. It can just be five or 15 minutes where you sit, focus on your breath and let go of your thoughts as much as you can. Breathe and let go, breathe and let go. That's it.

'I'm no good at sports'

We can all find an exercise routine that keeps our bodies alive and frees our minds. You might not find the right thing immediately and it can change over time, but there will be something out there for you.

You can trust me on this one! For the first 25 years of my life, I was convinced I was no good at sports. I thought the world was divided into people who were naturally good at sport, and those who were not. I was firmly in the latter group – that was, until Jose Luis helped me to see that this belief wasn't serving me. He literally took me by the hand and we ran together – five minutes of running, followed by five minutes of walking, repeated twice for a total of 20 minutes. Gradually, we increased the time, and after a few weeks I could run for 30 minutes without stopping. Running became a huge part of my life and I would often go on solo runs. There was a time, when our daughters were younger, when Jose Luis didn't like me going running on my own. He felt it was time we could have been spending as a family, but once

I explained how the runs made me feel – balanced, calm and happy – he understood how valuable my runs were to me. It can be hard to negotiate acts of care for ourselves, but it is essential. Now, I run as much as I can – normally every day.

One of the reasons I love running is that it helps me process difficult feelings. As I run, I check to see if there is anything lingering that is making me unhappy, worried or anxious. I systematically organise these thoughts until everything feels more manageable. A good run often helps me to understand why I might be feeling off. In my work, I'll often hear stories that are very sad and affect me deeply. What helps me find my way back to the light is running. I've had tears streaming down my face on many runs and I've allowed them to wash over me. In those moments, I feel the earth beneath my feet, look up at the sky, and renew my commitment to do what I can to channel this sadness into passion to fuel my fierce. That restores me. I am so grateful that all those years ago Jose Luis helped me to start running.

Writing

I've never really kept a diary since I was a teenager, but I have always carried a notebook with me. In it, I write down thoughts, insights, quotes, conversations, ideas that mean something to me, and revisit them when I am in need of inspiration.

Three years ago, I started to write more regularly, creating a space where I could sit and let my thoughts flow. Sometimes I pose myself a question and reflect on it. I write until I know that I have reached an answer that resonates deeply within me. Melis Senova, who introduced me to this technique, told me that I would know when I got close because it would feel uncomfortable – it's so true! Sometimes I sit and I write down some reflections and they are fine, but I know I'm only scratching the surface and not really going to the root of the issue I'm trying to understand. Melis told me to keep writing until it starts to be hard. I see this as getting into the mud. When it gets heavy, you know you've reached a place where you need to do more work. It is not easy, but it works. I have gained incredible insights into my own behaviour patterns, triggers and beliefs as a result of reflecting on my feelings, beliefs and behaviours through writing. I cannot recommend it enough.

Searching inside of myself in this way is a deep form of self-care – in fact, my writings over the years have formed the basis for this book, and the fears to fierce journey.

Try something new (and be bad at it)

Giving ourselves the opportunity to learn something new is a sign that we know we are capable of ingesting new knowledge for the benefit of our future selves. If you are reading this and have always wanted to learn how to sew, tap dance or take a beautiful photograph – do it. Do it for yourself.

And here's the thing I have learned about doing something new and finding joy: you don't have to be good at it. How liberating is that? Ten years ago, I met a woman called Catherine at an event, and we both decided to start playing tennis. We were bad – seriously bad! So bad, in fact, that when we asked a coach to give us lessons, she told us we'd need to get a ball over the net and have a ten-shot rally before she'd even begin to consider helping us. But do you know what? I loved it. The great thing was that for every ball that ended up in the net, we laughed. In fact, we spent most of the first year on the court furthest away from any spectators laughing our heads off. We did eventually manage to get the hang of it, and ended up playing regularly. Now, we are good friends – and tennis partners.

Tennis taught me that when I manage to let go of my ego's attachment to perfectionism – where I have to be really good at everything I do – and replace it with an experimental mindset, I experience joy and a glorious lightness. A space opens up where I don't judge myself. Joy isn't always found only in the things we're good at. Sometimes, it's about giving something new a go and being surprised by the discovery of joy in an unexpected place. Now *that* is great care.

Being outside your comfort zone doesn't always feel like great care because it can be uncomfortable, but eventually the benefits will show. In *Feel the Fear and Do It Anyway*, Susan Jeffers encourages us to try one thing every day that makes us feel a little uncomfortable. When I read her words for the first time, they made so much sense to me. If we only do what we feel comfortable with, our world will not expand. In fact, it will contract, because we will focus more and more on fear and we might even stop doing things because the fear will fester. But if we show ourselves that we can feel fear and do it anyway, it becomes less scary. **Developing the habit of doing one thing a day that is uncomfortable is an amazing care commitment.**

Get the dog

For years, I dreamed of having a dog to run alongside me on my morning jogs. And it wasn't just me – every person in our family wanted a dog. But we always focused on all the reasons why we *couldn't* have one. It was only when I allowed myself to focus on all the reasons why having a dog would be good for us as a family that something shifted. Five years ago, Emma was doing her GCSEs; I wanted her to take regular breaks and get outside. And, as Emma and Sara were growing up, I was aware that having family time was becoming difficult. I thought a dog would get us all out on walks together. I had also read *The Sweet Spot* by Christine Carter. In it, she speaks eloquently about the danger of overwork and how her dog would regularly come and ask her to play, naturally forcing her to take breaks from her desk.

I focused on all of these reasons and we started looking for a puppy. A week later we had found a breeder and we went to choose our new dog. Bruno is now nearly five years old and is currently sitting on my lap as I type. I am not exaggerating when I say that he changed our lives. He made us go for family walks, helped Emma stop studying every so often, and made us all happier. Even in the grumpiest of times, Bruno makes us smile and lifts our mood. I am forever grateful that I found a way through the fear and worry about how we could fit a dog into our lives because it helped us access the joy and love he brings us now. It took a while to train him to run well with me, but now he is my morning companion every day. And because we wanted Bruno to have a companion too, we got a second dog, Lola.

My dogs have shown me that what we might think is impossible is not always so. **When we stop focusing on the reasons why something is not possible and tune in to why we wanted it in the first place, we open up a space where we can create changes that are good for us.**

So 'Get the dog' is my way of saying: Do that thing you've wanted to do for ages, but always told yourself you couldn't. For you, this might not be a dog. But the same principle applies.

Go away on your own (yes, really)

Before I get started on the life-changing benefits of taking a solo trip, let me just say this: I know this isn't possible for everyone – in fact, it's a privilege. But if you can make the time and funds available for a trip away on your own then do.

A few years ago, my friend and colleague Shivonne, with whom I now co-lead Women for Women International UK, went on holiday to Lanzarote on her own. For two weeks, she tried a new kind of sport every day, read feminist anthologies and chilled out. I remember her telling me about it and thinking that there was literally nothing I would like to do more than what she had done. And yet – I would never allow myself to do it, because I already travel for work and I know my family don't like it when I am away, so I feel I can't ask for it. That said, why shouldn't I be able to do something just for me? Going away on my own didn't make me a 'bad' person.

Well, as I sit here, writing this, I am in fact away on my own! When I got this book deal, I had a reason to seek solitude: I needed the space and time to write in peace – true space for concentration away from any distractions. And do you know what? Things haven't fallen apart.

And I have been restored in ways that holidays have never quite managed. When you are away on your own, all you need to focus on is YOU. You get to do exactly what you want and need. You don't have to ask for permission, fit in, compromise, negotiate or justify. If you want to wake up in the middle of the night and read: you can. If you want to sleep in and laze about all day: you can. You get to tune in to your needs and wants. By prioritising yourself in this way, you are signalling to yourself that you are serious about your commitment to your own wellbeing.

Celebrate yourself

When did you last celebrate yourself? Not for your birthday, or for passing an exam, or because you gave a good pitch to a client, but simply because you exist? In my experience, stopping to celebrate ourselves just because we're worth celebrating can have transformational results, but it can feel hard at first. One of the wonderful women I coach started by buying herself the occasional bunch of flowers for £20. She had initially planned to spend £50 on her flowers but she got cold feet and couldn't justify it, so settled on £20. That thought process in itself got her properly assessing how she valued herself. She went on to treat herself with a beautiful necklace. Whether it's a necklace or a perfume or whatever else, the point is not about how much money you spend. Rather, it's the symbolic value of deciding that you deserve it. For someone else it might be taking half a day off work and walking through fields on your own, or watching a movie at the cinema in the middle of the day with no one else around. Paying attention to what we think we deserve and what we think is justifiable when it comes to celebrating ourselves is important, because it will teach us a lot about what we think of ourselves and help us re-commit to our journey.

Knowing what doesn't work for you

As you begin to discover the care actions that resonate with you, you'll also uncover those that don't, which is just as important. It is often hard to know what saps our energy and brings us down, but growing awareness of these things means we can get better at avoiding them, or at least prepare ourselves to face such people or situations in ways that protect us. After all, no amount of running will truly rid you of people and situations that affect you in an unwanted way, but taking action when it comes to these parts of your life can be the most radical act of care for yourself.

Tuning in to my body and understanding which people and situations pep up my energy, compared to those that bring me down, is revealing. This knowledge helps me take important decisions about the direction of my life: which jobs to choose, places to go, friends to spend time with.

For the last few years, I have been working with a small team of volunteers to set up an office for Women for Women International in Germany. I had the original idea six years ago when Preeti Malkani, an entrepreneur from Hamburg who had read about Women for Women International in *Red* magazine, contacted me. She was inspired by the stories of women rebuilding their lives after conflict and wanted to help set up Women for Women International in Germany. I was excited and in turn inspired by Preeti and her entrepreneurial spirit, her drive and tenacity in reaching out to me after having read the article. As you know by now, that's what it's all about!

My energy was lifted. We set out to develop a business plan and a proposal for a German subsidiary for the US headquarters to consider. It was met with hesitation. The organisation was facing other challenges and it was deemed that the time was not right to divert resources and effort into setting up something new. I expected to meet resistance, but I hadn't anticipated an outright 'no'. I saw this as a unique opportunity to open up a new market, invigorate the global organisation through growth and ultimately help more women. I was extremely disappointed and my energy dipped, but I had to accept the decision and move on, while holding on to my vision until the time was right.

The opportunity came a few years later, when the UK public voted in favour of Brexit. Suddenly, having a European subsidiary that could continue to give the organisation access to the EU, the largest donor of development aid in the world, felt more urgent. I presented the idea again and this time I was given the green light to develop a full proposal for why the organisation should open in Germany. Over the next few months, I spent hours talking to lawyers, exploring different legal options and developing drafts, until we finally got sign-off from the global board. Then, the fun began. We were able to start talking about and promoting the work of the organisation in Germany, and began to grow a movement of women and men who were passionate about helping.

Observing my energy levels during the different phases of setting up the new entity showed me that I thrive in start-up situations, working closely with a handful of committed and inspired people to create something out of nothing. It took me right back to the beginning, when I started in the UK with my small team. It makes my heart race, gives me unlimited strength and energy, and I feel I could climb mountains. On the other hand, having to present lengthy papers and sit through bureaucratic meetings that aren't strategic brings my energy down. Both were needed for the successful setting up of the office.

There are two important points here. Firstly, even when we know what is not energising to us, we might still need to do it, but being aware of it helps. When we don't understand why we feel less energetic, that can affect all areas of life. Whereas when we know, we can be conscious and get on with it as a task that needs completing, without it affecting the joy in other areas of our life. The other point is that knowing what does not bring us joy means we can use this information to help us make informed future choices. **Care for yourself is also about making choices that will help you feel good and keep your energy high.**

The same goes for people. My most personal example of this dynamic involves a close family member, from whom I am estranged. I believed wholeheartedly that the person and I could have a fruitful relationship, if only I tried hard enough and could make them see who I was, what I needed, and how open I was to engaging with them. Nonetheless, at the moment, we can't. It's been one of the hardest lessons I've learned in my life but, eventually, I came to accept how I felt. I chose to look after myself. If the only relationship that person and I are capable of having at the moment makes me sad and brings my energy down, I need to protect myself, because **if I don't look after myself, no one else will.**

Because that's the thing about care: as much as most of us like to look after those around us, no one is capable of caring for you as well as you can care for yourself. So now it's your turn. Please do not just read on without making at least one care commitment to yourself. Read through the actions below and revisit my toolkit and you'll find plenty of ideas. What really helps some of the women I coach is to have someone who holds them accountable, or who they can report to on their care practice. Have a think about who could help you with this. One of the women I coach messaged me every day for a week on WhatsApp to tell me what she had done just for herself on each day!

Respect what your fierce is telling you about what you need – and then act on it.

Lessons learned

You cannot care for others if you don't care for yourself.

Caring for yourself means investing in your most precious asset.

You can create your own boundaries and look after yourself.

Trying something new is a powerful care commitment.

A care toolkit is a great resource: try meditating, writing, running – whatever works for you.

Not using your care commitments as a stick to beat yourself with needs to be your top care promise.

Care for yourself when with people and in situations that bring your energy down.

Actions

There are so many things you can do to start bringing care for yourself into your life – some I have spoken about above and give below – but this is by no means an exhaustive list. Perhaps the most important action for you is to stop, notice and tune in. Ask yourself what looking after yourself looks like.

- **Identify your needs**: What do you need for yourself to feel better in your body, mind and heart? What brings joy to your fierce? For me the simple act of stopping when I feel the sun on my skin, closing my eyes and being grateful makes a big difference. Becoming more aware of what brings you joy is a big step in your care practice.

- **Be kind to yourself**: Remember that sometimes the greatest care is not being harsh on yourself. Never use your care commitments as a stick to beat yourself with.

- **Deep breaths**: Try taking three deep breaths, three times per day. I hope you find it easier than I did!

- **Try meditation**: You can start with five minutes per day. Or just sit for a few minutes every day, noticing your breath and how your body feels. Try downloading an app that can accompany you. I use Headspace, but there are many others, including Calm and Insight Timer. Talk to your friends and find out what they do.

- **Reflections**: Use your notebook and pen to write down your thoughts and feelings. As I described above, it might take a while for you to get to the real bits that are waiting to be uncovered. Keep writing until it feels 'sticky'. Asking a specific question can also help, as we did with the beliefs work in chapter 4. When we formulate a question, we are proactively inviting answers. Sometimes they will come there and then; sometimes the answers will appear after days or weeks. But in my experience, every time I ask a question, I will eventually find the answer.

- **Do something new**: What was the thing that came to your mind when you read about the power of doing something new? Say the thing you have always wanted to do out loud now and start the process of getting you to the place where you will do it: book it, pay the deposit or tell a person who will hold you accountable. But do it now. Then message me on Instagram @britafs and tell me about it!

- **Find your exercise**: Give yourself time to find out what exercise routine works for you.

- **Watch your energy**: Think back to a time where you met up with someone and afterwards came home feeling exhausted. Ask yourself why that is. Next time you meet that person, remember how they made you feel. Ask yourself what you can do to minimise the person's impact on you. Remember to breathe and see which of your care practices might help you here. Chapter 8 will talk more about protecting your power.

- **Be accountable**: Find someone to whom you are going to be accountable for your care commitments. Report to them daily, or as often as you can. Remember this is like building a muscle and it will take persistence to make care a habit.

- **Add another human to your boardroom in your heart**: Let this be someone who inspires you because of how they care for themselves.

PART III

Transform Your World

Chapter 8

Impact

You matter

'Forget everything you've heard – your too much-ness is a Gift; oh yes, one that can heal, incite, liberate, and cut straight to the heart of things. Do not be afraid of this Gift, and let no one shy you away from it. Your too much-ness is Magic, is Medicine. It can change the world.'

– Ev'Yan Whitney, 'The Too Much Woman'

How to grow your impact

In a more conventional book, this chapter would be called 'Find your leadership style' or 'Become a more effective leader', but to give it one of those titles would be to exclude those who don't see themselves as conventional leaders. We are not conventional, and this is *Fears to Fierce*, so this chapter is all about YOUR impact, whether you hold a professional position of leadership or not.

Remember: we *all* have power and we *all* have impact.

Often, when we talk about impact it is in a business context: how do we measure the impact of this campaign? How do we make sure this project has a tangible impact? We hope that 'impact indicators' (such as SMART – specific, measurable, achievable, relevant and time-bound) will tell us when our business has achieved the impact we were aiming for. However, this perception of impact and the corporate focus on 'measuring' it is driven by a 'left brain' way of understanding, which tends to be analytical, logical and objective, as opposed to the 'right brain', which is more creative, emotional, subjective, intuitive and visual.

When I talk about impact, I am interested in the kind of impact that includes both the easy-to-measure and the less tangible. Inspiration, for example, is hard to measure, and yet it is one of the greatest propellers for change that there is. When someone inspires me, they can have a profound impact on me, but it's hard to encapsulate what the impact of that feeling is. As the writer Maya Angelou said:

'People will forget what you said, people will forget what you did, but people will never forget how you made them feel.'[22]

Self-awareness and setting intentions

Do you know how you make people feel?

Do you know how you want them to feel?

The answers to these two questions are the key to growing your impact. The first one requires you to grow your self-awareness – understanding how you *make* people feel. And the second asks you to be deliberate in your intention – how do you *want* people to feel?

As you hone both of these elements, you transform and grow your impact. While you do this work, remember what you

[22] As quoted in 2003 March 25, Carolina Morning News, Section: Bluffton Bulletin, Column: Beautiful Bluffton By the Sea, Spring Has Sprung Around Town by Carolyn Bremer, Page 3, Newspaper Location: Georgia. (NewsBank Access World News)

learned in the previous chapters: to trust, love yourself uncondi-tionally, focus on your strength and care for yourself.

Ultimately, you get to decide the impact you want to have. You are here now. You know your purpose, own your power and are free to be who you want to be. As you proceed, try to follow your fierce, because when your actions are guided by your fierce, you will make people feel what you feel, and they won't forget that.

Nurturing self-awareness

I want to tell you a story about how I came to understand the connection between self-awareness and impact. It was 3 September 2008, the day after my birthday, and I was starting my new job for Women for Women International. The organisa-tion had been registered as a charity just 18 months before and it was my task to help build it up in the UK. Over the next few months, I hired staff and set up the basic office infrastructure, systems and processes. I loved working in this start-up environ-ment and usually appeared bright and joyful, but it was intense. There was a lot to be done and, on some days, balancing a new, exciting and demanding job with my family life was tough. At times I felt exhausted and it was hard to come to the office with an enthusiastic smile. I didn't think this was a problem – after all, we can't be happy all of the time.

It wasn't until six months into my job that my new office manager, Kate, mentioned to me that the way I turn up in the office impacted everyone else. She described how I would lift everyone up when I arrived with a bright smile and a refreshing 'Good morning', how my energy was infectious and motivated everyone to work harder. In the same vein, she said that when I was not my usual self, it really affected the whole team.

I had managed teams before, but maybe because I had never been the most senior person in an organisation, or perhaps had never had staff brave enough to tell me, Kate's confession made a big impact on me. I had not appreciated that everyone's eyes were on me, or fully understood the responsibility I was carrying. This responsibility was not written down in my job description, but it was critically important to the success and satisfaction of my team. I was not aware enough of the power I held and the impact I made.

This meeting started a journey of getting to know my impact and becoming comfortable with it. It is one of the hardest things I have done (and I'm still doing it every day), but it's also been transformational. What Kate told me stayed with me and I gained a new awareness of myself. I started to observe how my presence would shift the energy in a room, how staff responded to my cheerful greetings. I saw what Kate had told me: when I was feeling good, staff would sit up a little bit more, a smile would appear on their lips, as if a little summer breeze had swept through the office and everything seemed a little lighter. I also appreciated that it must be hard for the team to understand when suddenly there were days when I didn't appear like that. They worried, took it personally, or assumed they had done something to cause my change in mood.

Now that I understood, I made two commitments to myself: firstly, I would be more aware of the impact I had on my team and honour, treasure and take responsibility for it. Secondly, that it was okay for me not to feel great at times, but that I would then communicate to my team the reasons for it; or if I did not feel comfortable explaining myself, I would keep quiet and appear as my usual self. Letting it hang out without an explanation was no longer an option and I now also try to employ these same commitments with my family and friends. I try to be mindful of the impact I have on them.

Importantly, this behaviour has also become one that I encourage in those around me. Whether you're in a 'top' job or not, **there is always someone watching you, learning from you, looking up to you, worrying about you if there appears to be something wrong with you.** That is the reality.

Becoming more aware of your impact will help you to own your power in a way that feels true to you – in other words, in a more authentic way. Commit to being aware at a forthcoming meeting you have scheduled. Afterwards, ask yourself how you appeared. What did you say, do and think, and how did the other person(s) respond? Why do you think they responded in this way, and what is it telling you about yourself, about the impact you had on them?

The signs might be small. You might walk in and notice how the other person sits up taller and starts smiling, or that they begin shifting in their seat and looking down nervously. Whatever it is, they are all signs that can help you become more aware of your impact. Sometimes we shy away from being more self-aware, because we are not comfortable owning our power. As you go deeper here, allow yourself to sit with these questions and come back to them. The answers will not be easy and might take time.

As you complete the other self-awareness exercises in this chapter's action plan, you will continue to become more familiar with your impact and, I have found, want to grow it. In fact, the more aware and comfortable you become, the more your impact will grow. But you can have an even greater impact by being deliberate about how you come across.

Setting intentions

Setting intentions is the act of trusting your power and directing it in order to create the impact you want. It's a practice I use to give my awareness a direction, and I think you're going to love it.

Before I share some exciting examples that will help you set intentions, a note to remind you that the kind of impact we're interested in is holistic: that is to say, it taps into both our left and right brains, and our fierce. This isn't always easy to hold in our minds when we're defining the impact we want to have because we have been conditioned by a patriarchal society that puts greater value on the left side of the brain, which tells us our impact should be measurable and rational. As we think about the impact we want, let both the left and right brain in. We are clever *and* emotional because our power comes from both. The impact we want to create is not 'just' at work, it is for our full life.

I discovered the importance of setting intentions a while ago. A good example of this is the work I did with my team two years ago, as Women for Women International hosted its first feminist festival aimed at younger women. The team had worked for months on bringing together a fantastic line-up of inspirational, diverse speakers, and the agenda was brilliant – all the elements were there. We had set a target for how many young women we wanted to have there on the day, how many free spaces we would offer, how many speakers we needed, and so on. We had defined what our measurable impact would be.

Importantly, we also set clearly defined non-measurable impact criteria we wanted to achieve: all speakers should speak authentically, emphasising their own feminist journey and highlighting the pitfalls; everyone in the audience should feel inspired, included and empowered; everyone involved in organising the event should behave in an authentic, vulnerable and open way. We wrote those points down and shared them so that everyone was clear about our intentions, and how to support them.

And it paid off. The feedback from the festival was astounding: 92 per cent of the audience who filled in the evaluation said that they loved the event. Many spoke about how it had made them feel – using many of the words we had included in our intention setting. Alongside the ticket sales or margins, to me, this was what success looked like. To this day I still get stopped on the street and asked when we're going to organise another feminist festival!

Setting intentions can work for anything you do: a conference like the one I was describing, a job interview, a difficult conversation with a family member. It doesn't mean the event or conversation will always go the way you've intended, but it will be infinitely more likely, because you have worked out exactly what you are bringing to it and why you are there. That is all you can do – the rest is out of your control – meaning you'll be free to use your remaining energy to understand the other, read them, sense where they are coming from and respond from a place of authenticity.

Take a job interview, for example. Any interview is nerve-racking because the dynamic is designed to test whether we are 'good enough' for something, which taps into one of our deepest fears: *not* being good enough. Recently, I had an interview for a voluntary trustee role. I really wanted the position because I was keen to contribute to the organisation and learn from their experience.

As I prepared for the interview, I spent time learning about the organisation, understanding what they were looking for and matching that with my CV and interests. Then, I set my intentions. I thought about how I wanted to be in the interview and wrote it down: thoughtful, calm, measured, committed and serious. I had chosen those words in line with the role and the organisation. For a different role I might have chosen to focus on other parts of my authentic self. When people tell you to just be yourself in an interview scenario, their advice is only partially useful. In fact, you should be YOU – but in relation to the impact you want to create in that specific role. Your intentions need to take into account what you know about the entire situation: the organisation, the interviewer, the position you want.

After setting my intentions for how I wanted to be in the interview, I did the same for how I wanted the interviewer to feel: listened to, understood, connected to me and my authentic self.

Finally, I made a commitment to myself to stay alert and self-aware throughout the interview so that I would learn as much as I could. Those moments of stress are always amazing teachers. Besides, that way, if I didn't get the role, it wouldn't be a failure or waste, but an opportunity to practise and learn. After all, if I knew I had brought all I could to the interview and it didn't work out, it wouldn't be because I was in some way 'wrong', but because the opportunity wasn't right for me. If we approach interviews as chances to learn more and not tests of whether we are good enough, we shift away from valuing ourselves through the eyes of others, and instead we focus on what is within our power.

Don't be attached to the outcome!

This is possibly the hardest part. So, you've set intentions but you have to disregard the outcome? Yes! Why? Because our commitment to grow, evolve and look after ourselves is bigger than one or two singular scenarios and because we create an impact along the way, even if the outcome is not what we expected.

In Michelle Obama's autobiography *Becoming*, she discusses how she and Barack used what he had learned from working in community mobilisation in his presidential campaign. She writes so compellingly about how the very process of setting up and developing his campaign was creating fundamental and lasting changes in communities – that even without winning the elections, they were leaving a legacy, having an impact.

If we become obsessed with our intentions, they will not serve us. For that reason, I set the intentions, and then I let them be. I trust that I know the direction and stay alert and aware to observe what happens along the way. Becoming too attached to intentions is equivalent to exerting control over ourselves, which will lead to frustration. **We cannot control how others perceive our power; all we can influence is how aware we are, how we intend to proceed, and how we lead ourselves.**

If you are curious about the outcome of my interview, don't worry – I would be too. But I have omitted it because, for the purpose of this exercise, it's irrelevant: I was clear about my intentions for the process and the impact I intended, and that is what matters. Whether or not I got the role is not the point!

Writing this book is another great example of this. I spent a significant amount of time thinking about my audience, who you are and what you might need and want. I set clear intentions for my voice, how I want to communicate with you, and how I want you to feel as you read this book. How you will actually feel is outside my control, so now that I've done all I can, I have to let go and trust.

Ultimately, **setting intentions is the act of directing your power towards the impact you want to create, which in turn fulfils your purpose.** You see, it all comes full circle!

So set some intentions now. Perhaps think about something that is really important to you – an upcoming meeting, an event or a conversation. Ask yourself how you want to be for that moment. How do you want to feel? How do you want the other people to feel? Use what you know about yourself and your power. Try to visualise yourself in that moment. Close your eyes and see yourself, feel how you will feel if you realise your intention. The clearer you can sense your intentions, the more powerful they become. You will then remember them more easily in the moment. You can also write them down, or draw a picture that further visualises your intention.

The greater our awareness, the clearer our intentions, the more direct our impact will be and the greater our power becomes. But as we become louder with our power, discomfort is likely to creep in. After all, being powerful and using that power is quite exposing, and if you're not used to that, it can be scary. We will need to dig deep to transform and move through fears to fierce!

With power comes the stage

Over the past 11 years, I have given everything in my power to grow Women for Women International. I committed to my own growth and power because I knew that as I grew, so would the organisation. I embraced the notion of being the change I wanted to see and trusted that my self-leadership would create change and help the organisation fulfil its mission of helping women in countries affected by conflict.

As I learned to live with and use my growing power, I could see that I was having an impact on the organisation, and that, in turn, the organisation was having a greater impact on the women it was helping. As a result, my power was growing, and so the circle continued. Then a few years ago, I noticed I was being approached more and more as Brita, a human who had undergone transformation and from whom people wanted to hear, not just as Brita, Executive Director of Women for Women International.

That presented a new challenge for me. Up until then I had seen my power as being in service of the organisation and that helped me feel okay about having it – it justified my power. But now, something had shifted. Being asked to speak as *me* forced me to revisit deeply held beliefs I had about power: that it is inherently patriarchal, hierarchical, dangerous, corrupting, and will always be abused. In all honesty, I feared it.

Too often, I had seen people become intoxicated with their own power, losing themselves in it and forgetting their purpose. Their lives became about holding on to power, not about the good they could do with it. Many of the politicians I have seen rise from humble beginnings to positions of real power are perfect examples of this.

I had always been wary of the power I held as an executive director, but I had accepted it as part of the responsibility that came with the job. But this now was about me – as Brita, with my power, my impact. I felt uncomfortable, and I want to share with you how I managed to make peace with owning my power, by owning my impact.

Three years ago, Sam Collins, the same woman with whom I'd written my purpose statement eight years earlier, asked me to give the opening speech at her Aspire Women's Leadership

Conference. The audience comprised 500 professional women looking for inspiration and practical tips on how to take that next step in their career. She wanted me to reflect on what I had learned, how I got to be where I was in my life and career and share advice.

I was honoured, of course. But I was also scared.

I had two main worries. Firstly, that all too familiar fear: 'I am not good enough'. Would my experience be relevant and meaningful? Secondly, I was uncomfortable with being the authority figure bequeathing advice to all of these women; the person with the 'power'. Surely that would create distance between the audience and me? Besides, I didn't want to pretend I'd figured it all out, and deserved to be on a pedestal preaching about how they could follow in my footsteps.

The latter feeling stems from my belief that we do not help each other if we create separation; if we pretend to be someone we are not. I know that I connect most when the other person is human, vulnerable, fallible, real. That is how I wanted to be and I couldn't equate that with standing on a large stage talking *at* an audience.

I decided I would start my presentation on stage and then, after two minutes, walk through the audience, standing in different places to deliver different parts of my speech. This was my way of getting close to the audience and sharing what I knew in a way that felt authentic to me. In the run-up to the speech, I felt happy – content in the knowledge that I had come up with a plan I believed in.

But halfway through my speech, Sam walked towards me and took me back to the stage, asking me to finish there. I did as she asked, but I felt let down by her. I had carefully thought through my presentation; I had a purpose and a clear process. Even though I knew her reasons came from a good place (it made it easier for the audience to hear me; she thought I was scared of the stage and wanted to support me), I felt that, by interrupting me, Sam had misunderstood me.

After the speech, women from the audience thanked me. I could tell I had connected with them and many commented on how much they had liked me coming down from the stage. Then, Sam and Gosia, another coach I knew who was also speaking at the event, took me aside and told me that next time I should stay on stage. 'You need to stop being the mother and be the queen,' they advised. 'Queens don't walk through audiences.'

Their feedback was like a punch in the stomach. I had felt so elated after the speech: relieved that I had got through it and buzzing with the energy I had received from the audience. I had worked hard to make it authentic and meaningful in order to help other women learn and grow. I didn't want to be the queen.

Their words hurt. Outraged, I didn't know what to do with them. 'We're just not on the same wavelength,' I told myself. We simply had different ways of seeing the world and different intentions for how we wanted to appear as 'leaders'. As much as I admired Sam and Gosia, I could also choose not to accept their feedback.

But I kept thinking about it. Something niggled. There was another part of me that wondered whether I was shying away from something that I needed to examine more closely. What was I scared of? Could I stay true to my desire to connect, be real and not abuse my power, yet be on a stage? Was there the potential for me to abuse my power regardless of where I stood? Had I let 'being on stage' become a symbol for the dangers associated with owning my power?

The answer to all of those questions was yes. Over the next few months, I came to understand that **power in itself is neither good nor bad, it just is: it is what you do with your power that matters – the impact you create.** So long as I always intended to use my power to fulfil my purpose and create the impact I wanted to see in the world, I did not have to fear.

Over the next year I had more opportunities to become comfortable with my power. I gave interviews, and, while I focused mainly on my work and the organisation, I was also asked more personal questions. **During this time, I worked hard to find my voice and define the impact I wanted to have.** I started using Instagram and saw that people were interested in me as a person, not as a job title. Still, the fear reared its head. Like a bacterium that festers, it metamorphosed: sometimes it told me that people would think I was ridiculous. On other occasions, I feared I would lose sight of my purpose and get obsessed with my power, my ego.

Throughout all of this, I was trying to give a shape to what leadership meant to me. I realised that one of the reasons Sam and Gosia's feedback had unsettled me so much was because they had both influenced my thinking. In many ways, I had aspired to emulate them, so their words had felt like a severe judgement. But as I was evolving, I discovered that I needed to find my own way, however lonely and scary it felt.

I felt that I was betraying my mentors; that, by disagreeing with them, I was not being sisterly. I think many women fear that disagreement equals disloyalty, but celebrating our diversity and supporting each other nonetheless is, in fact, a brilliant expression of sisterhood. Sometimes, I see my close colleagues become uncomfortable when they feel they have to disagree with me. I know they love me and admire how I lead myself, so I always reassure them that disagreement is fine; in disagreeing, we're carving out our fierce.

Here is the crux: you will have your own special way of leading yourself and impacting others. It won't be quite like anyone else's way. Of course, you'll be inspired along the way by other humans, and while you might adopt elements of their approach, you'll never find someone who you'll want to copy entirely. You have your own unique fierce, your own purpose guiding you to create your own impact as a leader. Think of it as your 'leadership alchemy': as you read this book and go on this journey, you're brewing your own mix of qualities through which you'll lead. There is no one who can do this for you. All the work, reflection and transformation you are doing by embracing the fears to fierce journey is an articulation of your leadership alchemy.

Look back over the notes you've been making as you've worked through the action plan in each chapter, and write down some words or phrases that you think represent your 'leadership alchemy'. Some of mine are compassion, clarity, loyalty, commitment to equality, embracing change and transparency. Each word or concept has deep meaning for me and I know why I chose them. Make sure your words are meaningful for YOU. Then, as always, consciously exercise them to create your desired impact. Identify the earliest opportunity to put your impact to the test. Do you have an event, or a meeting, a task or a call coming up where you can practise your leadership alchemy intentionally? Decide now when you will do this. Set the date. Commit.

As you proceed in your fears to fierce journey, you might be wondering what your impact will be. That, of course, depends on your purpose. If your purpose is to positively impact the environment, maybe you could start by presenting a proposal to your family/co-habitants for how your household might reduce the environmental impact of your consumption patterns. You will likely want to lead by example and show how you are leading yourself to ensure that your actions are consistent with your purpose. Or if your purpose is to ensure that young women living in the UK do not feel that their opportunities are restricted because of their perceived class or where they were born, you might use your personal social media accounts to talk about your own experiences.

Know that as you start exercising your voice and growing your impact, you will learn. You don't have to start as the perfect, finished article. Every day offers you the opportunity to learn something else about your fierce, what moves you, and how you can serve your purpose in your unique way. As you are trying different things, some will feel just right. Those you keep, and add to your leadership alchemy. Others will not feel quite right, those you can let go. Trust yourself, you will know.

Overcoming discomfort

Turning up the volume on your impact can feel exposing, and, when that change is visible to other people, you might feel scared. But discomfort is an inevitable part of the work we're doing, and fears to fierce is an ongoing commitment to face fear and choose fierce. The more you double down on this commitment, the more comfortable you'll become. I want to tell you about a few key lessons I learned as I went through this process myself:

1. I did not realise that my reluctance to claim my impact came from a deep belief that power always corrupts.

2. Defining my impact felt lonely. There was no one out there who was modelling the exact 'leadership' I wanted to deploy to create my impact ... so I was on my own.

3. I realised that authenticity is being in my power and being comfortable with it. But that can make others uncomfortable, which can be hard to deal with. Guess what? Not everyone will like it when you turn up your volume ...

4. Don't take responses personally – learn from them.

5. Most importantly, don't give up your power to make others feel comfortable.

Hold your power to achieve your impact

I still have moments when I'm uncomfortable with my power. I call them 'growing pains'; because I am constantly evolving, my power is too. One of the biggest challenges you will face is the reaction of others as you grow your impact. Some might even feel threatened, which could distract you from what you are trying to achieve.

As we become more authentic, owning our power and feeling comfortable with it, we stop making ourselves smaller and apologising for ourselves. We stand up tall, we smile, we feel strong in what we're doing. But when I went through this process, it unsettled some people around me. I hadn't expected this. I thought having an impact could only be a 'good' thing ... but I was wrong.

Some time ago, a colleague with whom I had worked for a while, and who had guided and supported me, was not able to cope with me growing my impact. That year I had done an intensive ten-month executive coaching course and the impact had been phenomenal. I remember other colleagues telling me that I was transforming at lightning speed, which was hard for them to keep up with. Suddenly everything was shifting; what they knew of me was not necessarily true any more. This was understandably unsettling. The colleague in question could not cope with my increased power and impact. It meant I did not depend on them as much, and this was clearly unsettling their role and therefore their sense of worth. Instead of acknowledging this, they lashed out and started to challenge and undermine me. I felt they were trying to make me go back to who I had been before.

I had to learn not to take those responses personally. I told myself that everyone is on their own journey; their words or actions are not a value judgement of who *I* am.

In fact, it was in those moments that I needed to pay most attention so that I could resist the temptation to relinquish my power and shrink my impact. It is easy to want to give up your power in order to make people around you feel more comfortable. As women, I believe, we are conditioned to want to make other people feel good right from our first breaths: to be good girls, good wives, good daughters. Tuning in to how others are feeling and adapting your own behaviour to suit them can feel like an innate reflex.

What is the worst fear you have attached to owning your power? Asking yourself this question is a good way to help address it. From my work with other women, I know that one of the most common fears we have is that we will not be lovable if we are too strong. But as we've learned, love that requires us to be small can't nourish us. We've also come to understand that we are stronger than we think, and we can trust that the right people will be able to love us as we own our power.

I'm not saying that in order to embrace our own power we need to stop being empathetic – on the contrary. But some of the biggest challenges we will encounter as we move from fears to fierce are the opinions of others around us. Recognising that this is part of the process and riding it out is one of the hardest things to do. But don't give up your power; it never works.

One exercise I use when I feel that others want me to minimise my impact and make me smaller is called 'Hold'. When I feel an urge to make myself small to please someone else, I repeat the word 'Hold' in my head three times. I breathe carefully and say nothing. Although the urge to say something to please the other person is overwhelming, it will come at a cost: giving up your power. Repeating 'Hold' will make the urge to placate subside. Then, observe how the dynamics of the space you are in change: if you can hold, you'll push through and create the impact you want to see. And there's more: not only are you holding on to your power, but in doing so, in not satisfying the other person's needs, you'll help them change their behaviour too. There are no guarantees, but they might just see that they don't have to challenge your authenticity and make you feel small in order to make themselves bigger. In this way, when we own our power, we invite the other person to do so too. This is your impact rippling outwards already.

Of course, there will be times when you can't stay in your power. That's fine: be kind to yourself, reflect on why you gave up your power, and remember the 'Hold' tool next time.

Two years ago, Sam asked me to speak at the same conference again, as the keynote speaker. I was excited because I had started working on this book and was planning on sharing my thoughts on self-leadership with the audience to see if they resonated. I was also excited because I was going to be on the stage – and stay on the stage. I was ready to own my power and trust that I could have the impact that I wanted. It felt very different as I was delivering my speech. I felt fierce and real. I was not scared, and I also was not the queen. I had found my own way.

Since then, I have had many opportunities to observe how my presence impacts other women to allow their own power to shine through. More and more women are asking me to coach or mentor them, believing that I can help them with their own transformation. By leading myself, embracing my power, I am inspiring others to do so too, which directly fulfils my purpose. Every time I have a coaching conversation, I hold the space for another woman to unfurl her power. Sometimes, I'll see inspiration literally shine through the other woman and it reflects back and inspires me. Remember, 'As I witness another woman's rising, she gives me wings.' That is the impact I want to create.

I am no longer fearful that my power will somehow envelop or corrupt me. Instead, I trust myself to be able to bear the responsibility. **With power comes the stage – you don't really have the choice.** You have to accept it. It's *how* you accept it and what you *do* with it that will be your impact.

Lessons learned

We all have impact.

We grow our impact as we become more aware of it.

We direct our impact by setting intentions.

We get to decide what we want our impact to be.

Power in itself is neither good nor bad. It is what you do with it that matters.

Authenticity is owning your power and feeling comfortable with it.

Actions

Practise self-awareness

- Think back to a recent meeting you had. When you arrived, what did you say, do, think, and how did the person respond? What sense did you get from them? How do you think you made that person feel? What did they do?

- Think about a meeting that you have coming up, or perhaps a date with your friend or partner, or maybe a shopping trip with your daughter – commit to being aware and observe your impact on that person. If you can, write it down in your reflection journal.

- Think about people who have given you feedback. What do they tell you about yourself? Does that resonate? If it doesn't, where is the dissonance? Can you reconcile it? Ask yourself why you think that people perceive you in this way when you don't think that is the impact you have?

Practise setting intentions

- Identify an event/conversation/meeting that you want to set an intention for. Ask yourself:
  - How do I want to *be* in that moment?
  - How do I want the other(s) to feel as a result of my behaviour there?
  - What do I want the outcome(s) to be for that moment?

Set the intention to:

- Make space for self-awareness during the event.
- Be detached from the outcome.

Visualise your intentions:

- Close your eyes and see yourself in that moment.
- Feel how you will feel if you realise your intentions.
- The clearer your visualisation, the easier it will be to call it up during that moment; writing it down or drawing something is also helpful.

Growing your fierce impact

- **Your beliefs**: What do you believe about power and its impact, and about YOUR power and its impact?

- **Your leadership alchemy**: Looking back over the notes you've been making as you've worked through the action plan in each chapter, write down some words that you think represent your 'leadership alchemy'.

- **Try it out and make a habit of it**: Identify the earliest opportunity to put your impact to the test. Do you have an event, or a meeting, a task or a call coming up where you can practise your leadership alchemy intentionally? Decide now when you will do this. Set the date. Commit. As soon as you have done it once, make a habit of it.

- **Embrace challenges**: The more you practise harnessing your impact, the more likely it is that you will start to experience challenges. Note when people feel challenged by your impact. Why do you think they feel challenged? What is it telling you about your impact, and about them? Try the 'Hold' exercise when you next feel your power is under threat.

- **Visualise your protective armour**: When you notice that challenging responses are getting you down, use this visualisation technique. Close your eyes and imagine you are wearing a protective armour; this can be whatever you want it to be. I visualise a gorgeous diamanté catsuit, which I wear when I know I am going to be in difficult situations that might make it hard for me to hold on to my power. It protects me and helps me keep hold of my power.

Chapter 9

Change

Together we embrace our shared humanity

'Rise for you
Rise for me
When you rise first
You rise for She.'

– Rebecca Campbell, *Rise Sister Rise* [23]

Fifteen years ago, I was on the London Underground on my way to work when a woman leaped through the closing doors and into my carriage. In the heat of the race, she lost one of her shoes on the platform; the doors had already closed when she realised what had happened. I could tell she was mortified and deeply embarrassed because everyone was staring at her, and I immediately felt for her.

At the time, I kept a spare pair of trainers in my bag because every evening, after work, I had to race across London on my scooter to pick up my daughters from nursery. I wanted to jump up and tell her not to worry because I had trainers in my bag and she could have them, but as soon as the thought entered my mind, my heart began to race. I froze and a wave of fear washed over me. If I did that, what would she think? What if

[23] Rebecca Campbell, *Rise Sister Rise* (Hay House, 2016)

she rejected me? But I really wanted to help her, so I made a deal with myself: if she disembarked at the next station, which was also my stop, I would offer her my trainers. The train pulled in, and I got up to leave. The woman also made for the door, hobbling on the one foot that still bore a shoe. I approached her and offered her my trainers. She looked at me, surprised, and gratefully accepted. Then, we went to Marks & Spencer together, where she bought herself a new pair of shoes.

I still remember this episode all these years later because I was shocked by how hard I had found it to overcome my fear of ridicule. How is it possible that my genuinely empathetic reaction and desire to help had been distorted in my head?

It's because we overthink.

When we feel someone's pain or joy, it doesn't take long for our brains to rationally evaluate the feeling. Our judgemental voice tells us to stop, that we're stupid, that there might be negative consequences to our actions. We tell ourselves that we don't know what that person is feeling, we have no right to intervene, however well-intentioned we are. And so – usually – we sigh, let go of the instinct to help and move on. In that moment we kill our hope and silence our fierce.

This chapter invites you to alter your path by following that innate feeling and allowing your fierce to guide your actions. Your fierce is a muscle that grows stronger with each action and, as you perform more small acts of kindness, you'll feel braver about engaging in bigger movements. In the previous eight chapters, we have looked at how we transform ourselves to lead the lives we desire and create the impact we want. All of this builds towards us becoming agents of wider, systemic change that will alter the structures, policies and politics that impact the lives of those around us – and this is what we'll focus on now. **It's about using everything we've learned to** act with our fierce for the benefit of our fellow humans, so that we may connect to our sense of sisterhood and shared humanity.

We are all activists, because we all have the capacity to take action.

Everything we have practised up until now – cultivating our self-leadership (chapters 3–7) and being less fearful of our power and potential impact (chapter 8) – has prepared us to let go of the egotistical voice and trust ourselves. **If we can trust our fierce, we won't question our impulse to help and connect with others.** And, as you'll see, getting through that fear is rewarded every time.

How does the fear that is stopping us from helping manifest itself?

Perhaps it's **fear of losing power**. If you're helping someone to gain power, for example, you might worry that in doing so you will lose yours. Two years ago, I asked Shivonne if she would co-lead the organisation in the UK with me. I was keen for Shivonne to step up because I didn't want to be lonely at the top. I don't see this as losing my power or influence – I have gained, and so have Shivonne, the organisation and therefore the women we serve. Making this decision also meant ignoring a **fear of ridicule** – another worry – because I knew that co-leadership was an unusual concept.

It can be **fear of danger** – that something will happen to you if you help. On a trip to Rwanda, I met women who hid the under-attack Tutsis in their homes to protect them from the genocide. They could have let a fear of danger stop them from helping, but they didn't.

It might be a **fear of losing out on experiences you feel entitled to**. I remember a story someone told me about a young person who had a disability, which meant the person couldn't participate in the annual class excursion. The school and the classroom teachers suggested changing the usual destination, a water park, to something more accessible. The mere suggestion that this class was not going to get the same experience as every other year caused uproar among many of the parents, so the school decided not to change the destination and the young person was forced to miss the excursion. All that was behind the unwillingness to help was the fear of losing out. It struck me at the time, when I heard the story, how short-sighted we can be when we are led by fear and in this case, entitlement. The other parents couldn't see that their children had the unique opportunity to do something different from the other classes. In fact, when we don't empathise, it is we who lose out the most.

Ironically, it's when societal norms are suspended due to extreme circumstances – a natural disaster, a war, extreme poverty – that people help each other more, even though the scenario means they probably have less to give than ever. I am convinced it is because they feel more connected to each other, less imprisoned by norms.

Less embarrassment, more empathy

Feeling deep empathy is at the heart of what propels us to action. It is an intrinsic human emotion, but one that we have learned to silence through social conditioning. If we can truly listen to our fierce, reclaim empathy and trust that our actions matter even if we don't know how, then we will act and change the world around us.

I believe that most of us are capable of feeling empathy, but many of us do not act on that feeling. So how do we move from the feeling of empathy to actually helping each other? And how do we develop that into taking action together for the sake of humanity?

Social conditioning discourages us from feeling empathetic towards each other. We are so preoccupied with boxing ourselves in, labelling each other good or bad, left-wing or right-wing, cerebral or practical. These labels then determine whether we deem the other person valuable, safe and worthy of our empathy.

When we leave social conditioning to one side and focus on our shared humanity, our instinct is to find something that connects us. Every time I meet a woman in another country, I intuitively seek to find our common ground. I talk to them about my daughters and ask about theirs. I speak about my husband and ask about their partner. I share stories about the food we eat. Once we feel connected, we are more likely to understand and help each other.

Have you experienced that? Next time you are in an unfamiliar situation, seek to find something in common with someone else there. You might have different jobs, but perhaps you have both lived in the same county, or maybe you both have a dog? I promise that once you have established a connection, you will feel more at ease, and the interaction will feel inspiring and enriching.

Throughout my working life, I have seen this again and again. I think of empathy as 'understanding by feeling'. Once someone has an emotional connection that allows them – however affluent – to see themselves reflected in the lives of those whom Women for Women International supports, they're able to empathise. Once they understand by feeling they will always want to help.

In turn, those who graduate from the Women for Women International programme have also helped women around them. I met a woman in Kosovo whose neighbour had been diagnosed with cancer and did not have the money to pay for an operation. She mobilised the women in her class, and everyone contributed a little. Together, they paid for the woman's treatment. When I spoke to her, she said to me that the greatest gift for her is to be able to help.

The power of sisterhood: I am you – and you are me

> '*We are the granddaughters of the witches they couldn't burn.*'
>
> – author unknown, quoted in *Rise Sister Rise*

When we are connected, when we understand by feeling, we realise that we are not really separate. We see our own humanity reflected in each other. Helping someone else is no longer an alien act, but an extension of looking after yourself, because you realise that if those around you are not well, you can't be either. Cultivating empathy and allowing deep connection makes us take action for our shared humanity.

I can feel your pain, without experiencing it. I can feel the pain of a nation that has experienced a genocide without experiencing it myself. We don't have to be the same to be one.

From an early age, I sensed that I could feel trauma and pain beyond anything I had ever experienced or witnessed myself. There was no rational explanation for it. The first time I remember feeling it was in Israel, when I was 11. We were visiting the genocide memorial, and I had the deepest, strongest feeling that I had been there before. It shook me to the core. I felt the profound inhumanity of the Holocaust. I felt that same depth of despair again when I visited Srebrenica in Bosnia in 2009, 28 years later. It took me straight back to Israel, to my 11-year-old self. This pain is in me, it is part of me, it is part of my fierce. I have since learned that there is a rational explanation for this phenomenon: epigenetics, a practice that studies the ways in which trauma can be passed on genetically across generations.

I feel pain for the violence and abuse women have been subjected to at the hands of a patriarchy that has treated them as second-class citizens for centuries. The legacy is deep, wide and painful. It is part of my experience and who I am. It is the pain of the 'witches' who were burned centuries ago; it is the pain of the Chinese women whose feet were bound. It is the women whose genitalia are being mutilated. It is the young girls who are being trafficked for the sex trade. They are me and I am them. We are part of womanhood, who has systematically been violated and abused.

Sisterhood, being aware of our shared humanity, is a feeling. We can tap into it. When we do, it becomes a way of being. You might not see yourself reflected in the strength of my feelings, but you will have your own personal triggers for that deep, expansive empathy – and they are what will propel you from feeling to action. When you are there, seek others who share your feeling, because together we are stronger. Together we are one.

Act on your feelings

Before we go on, I wanted to share a few ideas with you for how you can practise moving from 'feeling' to 'doing'. Set the intention that the next time you feel empathy rising within you, you will act on it. Say you talk to a colleague who tells you she's feeling unsure of herself, and you really want to help her by telling her about a book you read that she might find helpful. If the fearful voice in your head kicks in, put it to one side and tell it: 'Not today – I want to act on my feeling!' Sit down with your colleague and tell her about ... *Fears to Fierce*. Or maybe you pass a homeless person and think about stopping and saying hello, just for a minute. And so you do.

I have learned how powerful it can be to acknowledge another person. This can be with a smile, a gesture, a message, a letter. All of these gestures tell the other person: 'I see you.' Sometimes that can be the most powerful gesture, because whoever you are, it feels wonderful to be acknowledged.

It also helps to think about a recent occasion where you had the instinct to take action and then didn't. Maybe it was a letter from a charity asking you to donate. Did your instinct say: 'Yes, I would like to help them, this sounds good,' and then life simply got in the way? Go back to the letter now and do it. Acting on your instinct to help is a muscle you need to build up.

You can also nurture the feeling of sisterhood. Who comes to your mind when you think about sisterhood? Who do you feel deeply connected to? Do you see them regularly? Make time to see them because they are your sister, your cheerleader, and just being in their presence will help you on your journey.

Building movements for change

'Never doubt that a small group of thoughtful, committed citizens can change the world.® Indeed, it is the only thing that ever has.'

— Margaret Mead[24]

Thus far, this book has focused on helping us to find that feeling of sisterhood. Feeling inspiration, finding our purpose, investing in ourselves to fulfil our purpose by finding our power, trusting ourselves, knowing we are stronger than we think, cultivating love, caring for ourselves and then observing the impact of our power, understanding that, just by being, we impact others – **all that allows us to feel, to know that we are deeply connected and part of a shared humanity.** The fears to fierce journey will now focus on tapping into that feeling to forge the wider change we want to see in the world.

It is easy to forget that all change starts with one person, and then another and another until a movement is formed. There is a fantastic video on YouTube called *Guy Starts Dance Party.*[25] It shows lots of different groups of people sitting on the grass in the sunshine. Suddenly a man gets up and starts dancing. It

[24] Published by permission of the Mead Trust
[25] Sasquatch music festival 2009 Guy starts dance party (YouTube)

takes a while for a second person to join him, but gradually more and more people join until there is a huge dance party. I love this video because it teaches us a lesson about movements. It always starts with one person, and then another person deciding to join – and so on. And it is not just about the first person having a desire to dance, or the person with the idea, it is the second person saying, 'I will join,' and then the third. They are all key to the movement. Arguably the first person is as much a leader as the second one. Standing up for what you want – in this case dancing – is always your decision; it just gets easier when you are not alone.

On a freezing day in January 2017, I walked alongside 100,000[26] other people at the London Women's March. It was an unprecedented public demonstration in support of protecting women's fundamental rights and safeguarding the freedoms threatened by the recent election of Donald Trump as US president. In the words of the organisers of the Women's March: 'We united and stood together for the dignity and equality of all peoples, for the safety and health of our planet and for the strength of our vibrant and diverse communities. We came together in the spirit of democracy, honouring the champions of human rights who have gone before us. Our numbers were – and still are – too great to ignore, and the message to the world is clear: We're here, and we aren't going anywhere!'[27]

It was called the Women's March, but what made it so special was that it encompassed all genders and championed humanity, inclusivity and equality. For me, it was an incredible uprising: a manifestation of a collective power that brought us together, **connected in our differences and joined in our common humanity**. What's more, women were the engines.

[26] www.independent.co.uk/news/uk/home-news/womens-march-london-donald-trump-protest-trafalgar-square-inauguration-washington-dc

[27] www.womensmarchlondon.com

I had advocated for women's rights for over 20 years by that point and I had never been to such a large demonstration in the name of women and women's rights. Something fundamentally shifted that day – and continues to shift. In the early days of my career, people would laugh when I told them I studied women's studies, and worked for women's rights organisations, but those people aren't laughing any more. Suddenly it became acceptable to focus on the position of women in society. Enough of us had formed a critical mass to protest against the fact that over half the population is systemically treated differently.

That same year saw the explosion of the #MeToo movement denouncing sexual assault and harassment. I am certain that the unprecedented mobilisation for women's rights earlier that year contributed to encouraging so many people to use the #MeToo hashtag and speak out. The women who posted their stories knew they were not alone, which gave them courage. Whether you used the #MeToo hashtag to reflect a personal experience or you were one of the many women who were standing in solidarity, we were all outraged. This was our opportunity to join a movement that said no to violence against women. A year later, we saw #WhyIDidn'tReport spread, continuing and adding nuance to the public conversation. Survivors from all backgrounds used the campaign to focus on the powerful code of silence and shame that surrounds these crimes.

Scrolling through my social media feed at the time, what struck me most was that the stories of sexual harassment and assault could have been written by almost any woman, living in any country, of any class. I kept thinking of the many women I've met through my work. That same year I had spent time in Kosovo, Bosnia and the Democratic Republic of Congo – all home to large numbers of rape survivors. An estimated 20,000–50,000 women were raped during the Bosnian war, and 20,000 during the 16-month Kosovo conflict.

All the stories clearly demonstrated symptoms of deep gender inequality and power imbalances. The toxic mix of shame, guilt, trauma, fear and isolation that ran through each one showed so clearly that survivors carry the burden of the crime, often for decades afterwards, and often alone.

It made the coming together all the more powerful. This joining of forces by women has been at the heart of so much change. It reminded me of Leymah Gbowee, who spearheaded the Women of Liberia Mass Action for Change in 2003. From 1999 to 2003, Liberia endured a war that saw Muslims and Christians fighting each other, but after the war, Leymah united women from both sides. These were women who had lost their husbands and had to bear the pain of seeing their daughters raped and held as sex slaves. She said: 'We forged a sisterhood because our pains were similar.'

Speaking up is hard and loaded with fear – understandably so, because there has often been a terrible price for shining light into dark corners. But looking back, there have always been women who have spoken up: trailblazers, change-makers, pioneers, who have trusted their fierce, and together with others forged systemic change. Two decades ago, dozens of Bosnian women gave evidence during the first ever war crimes trial involving charges of sexual violence. As a result, rape was formally classified as a crime against humanity. Since then, more than 70 individuals have been charged with crimes of wartime sexual violence in the former Yugoslavia.

It is so easy to read these examples and be awe-inspired, convinced that they don't apply to you. It's that voice in our head telling us that this might be all well and good for these women but that's not us. In order to quiet that voice, remember that change always starts with one person and then grows. So **don't paralyse yourself by thinking about the big mountain. Think about the slope, the small hill that you will tackle now, and trust that the rest will come. It's all about starting.** Perhaps you passed that homeless person and stopped to speak to her, and she inspired you to do more. So you decide to tell your colleagues at work about her. Together you contact a local charity that works to support homeless people and start fundraising for the organisation. Every month, you and your team might even spend a few hours volunteering for the charity. And so it continues. Maybe, one day, you'll write a book about the stories of the people you met, and inspire so many more people to also care about homelessness. But remember, **the first step is always small, and it's one that you CAN take.**

Let me tell you about my friend, Lauri Pastrone. I first met her 11 years ago, when she called me at the Women for Women International office. She had been sponsoring women through the organisation's programme and wanted to do more. She loved cooking and wanted to compile her favourite recipes, alongside those from her friends, into a small booklet and sell it to raise money for Women for Women International. The key is that she had the idea – and then called me. She took the first step, a small step. And then it grew … From the initial booklet idea, four years later, a full-blown beautiful cookbook called *Share*[28] was published. It has sold over 50,000 copies worldwide, raised hundreds of thousands of pounds for the organisation and raised awareness of its work.

Between the first call and the publishing there were thousands of little steps, with many more people joining the project, creating an incredible impact. If Lauri had started with the idea of creating a cookbook with a foreword by Meryl Streep and recipes from Desmond Tutu, Nelson Mandela, Annie Lennox and Richard Branson, she probably would have opened a bottle of wine, laughed at herself and not done anything. So, remember, small hills, not big mountains – and then: trust.

Movements like #MeToo and #WhyIDidn'tReport can be life-changing for individual women and transformational for society. The more we look at examples of where we have joined forces to create the change we want to see in the world,

[28] Alison Oakervee, *Share: The cook that celebrates our common humanity* (Kyle Books, 2013)

the easier it will be for us to do the same. We need to inspire ourselves and remember what is possible in order to nurture communal hope. We need to know that when we come together, sometimes crossing what we think are unbridgeable divides, we are so much stronger than we think. Acting for the good of the world is the ultimate amplified expression of your fierce, and unifying with those who feel similarly to you will make it feel so much easier.

Abiola's story

Abiola, from Nigeria, is a brilliant example of a woman who has done just this. She saw her husband killed and her 10-year-old daughter murdered in a protracted conflict between her community (farmers) and the Fulani (herdsmen). She herself was shot in the shoulder, which has left her with lasting pain.

Abiola, a new widow and mother to four surviving children, the youngest of whom was just five months old, didn't know how she would feed her family. But while she was still in hospital, she heard about the Women for Women International programme and, soon after, she enrolled. Learning about trading and small-business management helped her to improve her livelihood. She was able to grow vegetables and start selling them at the roadside to passing travellers, earning her own money for the first time. She also learned about her rights and found her voice. Seeing how these changes improved her life made her want to do the same for other women around her: she wanted to grow her impact.

A force to be reckoned with, Abiola had embraced her own power. At that time, Women for Women International had recently developed a new programme whereby it supported a few women to create change in their communities. They were called 'change agents', and Abiola's class recommended her as a 'change agent'. She accepted, did the training, and has been advocating for women's rights in her community for the past two years.

Her impact has been exponential. In February 2019, the farmers and the herdsmen were still killing each other, but Abiola and her fellow change agents decided enough was enough. Wherever they looked, women were suffering, so they called a peace dialogue meeting with the support of the local authorities, and forged a peace agreement, which has been successful. As of spring 2019, the fighting has stopped, children have returned to school, the economic wellbeing of families has improved, women are safer and people who had fled the region are returning.

When I met Abiola in August 2019 she struck me immediately because she radiated joy and kindness, which is all the more enthralling when you know her story. Later, she, the other change agents and I were on a bus together driving to a distant community. Seeing them together made me realise the power of feeling part of something bigger. Earlier I had asked the change agents if they were scared about challenging rapists in their community. I knew that their actions directly infringed societal norms, and had the potential to put them in danger. But the change agents unanimously shook their heads and told me that they were not scared, because they were together.

As we drove, the change agents started to sing a song that they had made up. It was a beautiful song and the English translation of the chorus was 'Change agents we are together, we are one'. It moved me deeply to hear expressed so simply what I believe to be at the heart of creating the systemic changes we want to see.

When we arrived at the community, I was invited to attend the second round of talks aimed at recommitting to the peace agreement. It was a meeting initiated by the change agents, and male leaders from both sides of the dispute attended. Everyone spoke about what the peace meant to them. Men spoke about their appreciation for the changing role of women in the community, acknowledging that they had initiated the peace. I felt I was witnessing history being made. I know that women bear the brunt of conflict but that they can forge peace when they believe in their power and join with others. I also know that men can change their attitudes and be allies. Together, these things create long-term, sustainable change.

To think that Abiola not only found it within herself to forgive the killers of her husband and daughter, but became instrumental in forging peace by believing in her power and joining with others to create systemic change, is inspiring – individually, together, and for our shared humanity.

Inclusive movement, not exclusive club

Abiola and the change agents, along with many other women I have met, are all uniting across divides. We can learn so much from these movements led by women: the power of joining forces, yes, but also what to do with the backlash that can occur when we grow strong in numbers. As with our personal transformation, communal transformation will not always be welcome.

Almost as soon as the #MeToo movement began, it was criticised for taking the message 'too far'. This backlash didn't just come from people who felt threatened because it forced them to interrogate their own behaviour, but from other women too. In fact, at one point I didn't meet many people who saw #MeToo as a powerful force for change and progress. At the same time, I had started to follow how feminism, in some places, was becoming an exclusive club. In an era where being a feminist was becoming more acceptable, suddenly there were restrictions and criteria about who was allowed to call themselves a feminist and who wasn't cropping up everywhere.

Why do we work so hard only to limit and reduce our collective power? Why would we focus on what divides us, when there is so much that connects us? Why, when on the cusp of real change, do we revert back to our old ways of understanding power? It is because change is hard, painful and riddled with setbacks, and at the heart of it, I believe, is fear. If we are to harness the power of women, our sisterhood, and campaigns like #MeToo, the Nigerian peace process and so many others, we need to embrace a different approach, where we invite people into inclusive movements, rather than silo ourselves into exclusive clubs.

The key is to move away from dividing everything into neat, binary categories: right or wrong; love or hate; yes or no – where everything is always either/or. We don't need to be fearful or controlling. We can embrace diversity, complexity and difference. That then frees us up to focus on what we want to change. We can trust that our actions will make a difference and begin to grasp the wonder of life and humanity.

Success is never guaranteed, but we must try – with hope as our communal engine.

A new dimension

When we exercise this type of expansive empathy and act on it for the benefit of our communities, we open up a different world. Nurturing these behaviours paves the way for a paradigm shift, where the world as it is and the way that we live right now stops making sense.

You can do this. Search for others who share this feeling. By recognising yourself in others, you'll find the sense of belonging you have developed for yourself (as you'll have done in chapter 4). These people will become your tribe, and this new 'movement' of yours won't have norms and can't be understood in the context of the old paradigm. It will change and move and so will you. It will be non-hierarchical, movable, non-patriarchal – without a leader, but made up of many self-leaders like you and me. Movements like this transgress and transform.

Women are key for these movements because we can see how much we have suffered as a result of the current status quo and our fierce yearns for a different way. We know what is needed to restore humanity for the benefit of all. In this new dimension, fear is no longer the currency and our innate fierce is allowed to lead.

Lessons learned

We are all activists: once we practise taking action that changes our own lives, it's easier to believe we can also create wider change.

Feel empathy, and then act on it.

Trust your fierce; it's only fear that stops us from helping others.

When we help others, we feel a sense of connectedness, sisterhood and shared humanity. Allowing ourselves to see our reflections in the other, we understand that we are all one and then there is no room for fear.

Together we are stronger.

Hope is trusting that your actions will make a difference with no guarantees, and it is our communal engine for change.

Actions

This chapter has discussed the endless possibilities that open up when you follow your fierce and you take action to help others and join with them to create wider change.

Let me say this: whatever you decide to do is GREAT. Do not allow the voice in your head to belittle small acts because you are comparing them to Abiola's story. We are all different and we all have a role to play. Your actions might make a change in your community, or maybe they'll end up rippling outwards to a national or even global level. It doesn't matter – it's all needed – so commit to your fierce and don't listen to the judgemental voice in your head that seeks to criticise your actions and make you compare yourself to others.

Here's how to get started:

1. **Act**: The next time you feel empathy rising within you, act on it. Some scenarios might include:

   - Saying hello to a homeless person you pass in the street. Or simply look them in the eye and acknowledge them. Create a connection with someone you normally would not.
   - When you see a colleague struggling, and your instinct is to offer to help them, do it. Go up to them and ask if you can help them.
   - When you notice someone has been in the toilet for a long time and you think there is something wrong with them, follow your sense and ask them.

   All of these acts are powerful because they acknowledge the other person as important. **Think about what you didn't do.** Was there a recent occasion where you had the instinct to take action and then didn't? Go back to it now. Acting on your instinct to help is a muscle you need to build up. The more you do it, the better.

2. **Come up with your own ideas**: Start thinking about what you would like to do beyond that which is immediately in front of you (like a homeless person, or a charity letter). You can't help everyone, but you might decide to always help a certain group of people, or you could have a certain amount of change in your pocket for giving during the day and commit to using it up. Another way to help others

could be through mentorship. At any given time, I'll be mentoring three young women at the beginning of their careers. I give them one hour per month for six months – it doesn't sound a lot, but it's what I can afford to do around my other commitments. Use these examples as inspiration to help you find your own ideas about how you can practise helping others regularly.

3. **Nurture that feeling of sisterhood:** Learn to understand how you feel when you see your fierce reflected in someone else. Who comes to your mind when you think about that deep connection? Have you seen them recently? Make time to see them because they are your cheerleaders and simply being in their presence will help you on your journey.

4. **Make a list of causes you feel a connection with,** writing down why and what you would like to do for them. Identify your top one and get in touch with the people running it to find out how you might get involved. Even if you end up not becoming involved in that organisation, the act of reaching out will be a stepping-stone towards your activism. **The first step is always a catalyst that will guide you to a place where you are feeling your fierce, following your purpose and taking action.**

5. **Don't take no for an answer:** Whether it's the voice in your head, or the voice on the other end of the phone, do not take no for an answer. Trust yourself; you are committed to your purpose.

Chapter 10

Know

You are fierce

'And one day she discovered that she was fierce, and strong, and full of fire, and that not even she could hold herself back, because her passion burned brighter than her fears.'

– Mark Anthony[29]

There is one further element of the fears to fierce journey and that is the ability to believe something so deeply that I no longer question it; it just *is*. I call this deep knowing.

Knowing in this way is when we extend the trust we developed in chapter 4 to the world around us. As we lead ourselves with inspiration and purpose, when we trust, have strength, unconditionally love others and ourselves, care, grow into our power and impact and join with others to make wider change, we'll experience moments when we know deeply that we are exactly where we should be.

Open yourself up to these moments; they will appear like magic, like miracles, or perhaps 'weird coincidences' – they happen to me all the time now, but I remember that when they first started it felt super-strange. A few years ago, for example,

[29] Published on Instagram @markanthonypoet

I told my team at Women for Women International that I would love to involve Gillian Anderson in our work, because I could see what a committed activist she was, and I had read her book *We: A Manifesto for Women Everywhere*, which she co-authored with Jennifer Nadel, and seen many synergies in our work. We hadn't taken this any further, when one morning I was standing at the bus stop in King's Cross on my way to work. It was a rainy morning and I was feeling a little miserable, but as I was waiting for my bus, I checked my emails on my phone and, to my shock, I saw an email from Gillian herself. It said something like: 'Dear Brita, my name is Gillian, I am an actress and I would love to speak to you about Women for Women International. Can you call me ... ' It was a wonderful moment and reconfirmed to me that I was on the right path. When similar things happen to you, which they will, pay attention and use them to inspire you to choose your fierce.

When I think about the fears to fierce journey, I imagine a crossroads, where the signpost points towards fear in one direction and fierce in the other. You are so powerful that you can hold both the fears and the fierce within you. By now, you know both ways well. In this moment, you might feel as if you are balancing on a tightrope, knowing how much rides on the next step. Fear will always be waiting in one direction within you, but because you've nurtured your capacity to choose fierce it'll feel more available to you than ever.

That's not to say that the fierce path is easy. You'll always encounter more crossroads, and at each junction you'll be faced with a choice again. Do you choose fear, or reaffirm your commitment to your fierce? The fears to fierce journey is a never-ending one, but the more often you choose fierce, the easier it will be to do it when you come to the next crossroads.

Then, there are these magic moments – rewards, perhaps – that appear seemingly unexpectedly along the way. They'll give you the fuel to keep choosing fierce. These signs are when you KNOW. You'll feel a jolt of understanding, and everything you've learned in the past nine chapters will flash through your body, mind, heart and fierce! It's like an electric current of inspiration that fuels you.

You never know when these 'aha' moments might strike, you just have to be ready to see what they're trying to show you. To end this book, I want to share one of my most profound KNOW moments with you.

Amela's story

Women for Women International runs a sister sponsorship programme, whereby women in countries affected by conflict – Bosnia, Kosovo, Afghanistan, Iraq, Nigeria, DRC, Rwanda and South Sudan – are connected to sponsors, who we call 'sisters'. These are ordinary people, from all over the world, who want to help women rebuild their lives after the trauma of war. Inspired by the concept of global sisterhood, these one-to-one connections provide support and solidarity, as well as critical funds to support women through a year-long training programme.

This initiative was one of the key reasons why I wanted to join the organisation, and shortly after I was appointed, I signed up to sponsor a sister myself. Like so many others, I was excited by the opportunity to give back in such a personal and tangible way, so when I received an email introducing me to my 'sister', I was so excited. Her name was Amela and she was from Bosnia.

A few weeks after signing up to be a sponsor, I received a pack with information about Amela. She was a similar age to me and had two children, a boy and a girl who were close in age to Emma and Sara. The organisation encourages you to write letters to your sister to let her know that you are thinking of her.

Amela and I exchanged a few letters. This isn't always possible, but I was lucky that she had the means and language skills to write back to me. Around five months after I began sponsoring her, I received this letter from her:

Dear Brita,

Firstly, I want to ask you for the health of your family and you. Every time when I have a meeting with Women for Women International I am looking forward to receiving your letter. I decided to write to you again. Since this programme is about to end, I am hoping to get one of your long letters.

My country is currently covered with snow and it is so cold. My children enjoy each day and I spend most of my time in the house. I am not satisfied with all of it but it cannot be different. I am so happy because I got the chance to meet other women and because I had the opportunity to be part of the Women for Women International programme. This means a lot to me and it gives me the strength to continue living.

I must tell you that I used your donation to buy some flowers, red tulips. I will plant them and have you in my memory many years and every time I look at them. I am so happy that you know that I exist and that you think of me.

I will write down one recipe to you, so you can prepare this cake and invite your girls for coffee.

My family and I wish you all the best for the coming holidays.

Best regards,
Amela

As I stood at my kitchen table reading this letter, tears streamed down my cheeks. Emma and Sara, who were only nine and seven at the time, were visibly worried.

'Why are you crying, Mummy?' they asked.

'Don't worry,' I replied. 'Mummy is just really happy.'

That was all I could manage to say. I was moved so deeply that my breath felt as if it had been drained from my lungs.

I realised that I had this relationship the wrong way around. All the while I had thought *I* was giving, when in reality I was receiving. Receiving such love, appreciation and deep under-standing of our common humanity, and of how we can make a difference in ways that we would never imagine.

I am so happy that you know that I exist and that you think of me.

With these words, Amela expressed the essence of what had inspired me about the concept behind supporting a sister: one woman can make a difference to another woman simply by acknowledging her. We have such a huge impact on another person simply by saying:

'I see you.'
'I care for you.'
'We might never meet, but I believe in you.'
'I am with you.'

That single sentence inspired me so profoundly that I made it my leitmotif. For the next decade, I took Amela's letter with me everywhere. Whether I spoke at an assembly of sixth-formers in an all-girls school, presented to a group of investment bankers, met high-end beauty and fashion brands or lobbied government ministers, Amela was right there with me.

Five years ago, we launched a partnership with the jewellery brand Monica Vinader, who designed beautiful friendship bracelets which could be engraved with a friend's name. Mine read: 'Amela'. A year later, my team and I created a short film about Women for Women International's work called *The Women Behind the News Stories*. It started with a voiceover of Amela's words, alongside an image of her original letter in Bosnian and her photo.

I have lost count of the times I've seen people moved to tears by Amela's beautiful words, by the humanity of her message. In turn, that inspiration has led many to sign up to sponsor a sister and commit to our shared humanity themselves.

As you'll know from reading chapter 1 and following the fears to fierce journey, we feel inspired when something touches our heart. It ignites our fierce and it compels us to do something that is bigger than ourselves, that links to our purpose. That is why inspiration is a powerful force for change.

Down the years, as I told Amela's story over and over again, I dreamed of meeting her and telling her about the profound impact she'd had on me and so many others. Every time I travelled to Bosnia, I asked my team to try to find her. But with over half a million graduates worldwide, many of whom live in difficult circumstances, it is not always possible to maintain communication. Much to my disappointment, the team had been unsuccessful in their search for Amela.

Then, in September 2018, as I celebrated my tenth anniversary with Women for Women International, I was due to travel to Bosnia with a documentary team, who wanted to make a short film about the organisation's history in Bosnia and its ongoing work there. I decided to use this as one last opportunity to try to find Amela. It wasn't looking promising, but just days before we were due to leave for Sarajevo, the team in Bosnia told me that they had found Amela and that she wanted to meet me. To say I was thrilled would be an understatement.

My colleague Nermana picked me up from the airport, and we began the three-hour drive to Doboj, where Amela lives. Sitting in the car, my stomach churned with nerves and excitement. I couldn't quite believe that, after ten years, I was here in Bosnia, about to meet Amela, of whom I'd spoken so much that at times I worried that I had made her up! Nermana and I met up with the filmmaking team on the way and there was something special in the air. We could all feel it, it was infectious, and I knew I was not the only one with butterflies.

As we approached Doboj, I realised that I was worried. Had I made this special connection up? Surely there was no way this could be as unique and meaningful as I had imagined it. As my fearful voice tried to creep in, I endeavoured to calm down and remind myself that I should embrace the experience as it unfolded. This moment was for Amela and me, not the cameras or anyone else. We were going to meet because we were sisters.

Amela's house is right at the top of a mountain, at the very end of the last road in Doboj. We arrived at six o'clock in the evening, just as the sun was beginning to set. Amela had been waiting for us. She was standing outside her house as we parked. I got out of the car and walked towards her and we hugged. She looked different to the photo I had of her from ten years ago. Her blonde hair was cut in a bob and her slender figure dressed in a white t-shirt and trousers. We looked at each other and I could see my feelings reflected in her eyes. She spoke to me in Bosnian and even without the translator I knew what she was saying:

'I cannot believe you have come, Brita.'

I looked at her, taking her in. It was even more special than I had dreamed. She was my soul sister, my inspiration.

Inside her house, she took me by the hand and led me to her living room and through to a small balcony overlooking the valley. Bosnia is a beautiful green country and the hazy light draped the landscape in a soft glow that made everything seem all the more dreamlike. We sat next to each other, holding hands, unaware of the crew, translator and my other colleagues. Right in that moment it was just Amela and me. To say it was magical does not do it justice.

I handed Amela the letter she had written to me all those years before. 'Do you remember this letter, Amela? The letter you wrote to me about the tulips?' She nodded her head. Then, I told Amela about how I had carried her letter with me and read her words to so many people who in turn had been inspired to help other women. I showed her the film I had made, her letter and photo on the screen, and thanked her for providing the inspiration that had been my guiding light all along.

Amela wiped tears from her eyes. She told me that at school she had always liked writing, but her teacher had told her she was no good with words. To hear that her words had inspired so many clearly overwhelmed her.

'I have always dreamed and wished that, somehow, I might have an impact beyond just my own little world,' she said. 'That I might touch the lives of others. I never thought it would happen and now you have made it possible. It is my dream come true.'

Time stood still as I absorbed the simplicity of what she had said. **What moves us as human beings is the desire to have an impact, to know that we matter beyond our mere existence.** There are many things that I have learned from Amela and our connection, but above all **it is that we all matter.**

After I had told Amela about the far-reaching impact of her letter, Amela got up and pointed to the garden below the balcony. She told me that she planted the tulips there, and that they still flower every year. Hearing her say this felt unreal, to think that it was true that they flowered every year to remind her of me.

A year later, on my second visit, Amela and I went into her garden because she wanted to plant a flower I had brought her. As we kneeled on the earth, she started digging. I wondered what she was doing. After a while she stopped and pointed to the bottom of the little hole she had dug. There, in the soft soil, was a tulip bulb.

If I'm honest, when Amela told me that the tulips still bloomed every year, I hadn't been sure whether to believe her. It sounded too perfect, too symbolic, to be true. Nonetheless, I told myself that, in any case, it didn't matter. Now, I could see the evidence for myself. Looking at the bulb was an unspeakably humbling moment. I realised that I had still been questioning the impact of the work I had been doing and how it relates to our shared humanity. For all the learning and growing and choosing my fierce, I had still questioned whether *I* mattered. Seeing the tulip bulbs changed that. When I saw them, I knew that I did. I had tears in my eyes again, just as I had over a decade ago when I first read her letter.

We all have an impact just by being *who we are*. We might not see the evidence for a long time, or even ever, but we MUST believe it. If I had never found Amela to meet her in person, I would never have been able to tell her about the impact she had, and I would never have known the impact I had. We cannot always know the effect we have on others, and on the world around us, but we must know that we DO have an impact. Amela proved to me that this is true. As you can imagine, meeting Amela was life-changing for me because it reaffirmed that the inspiration I had felt all those years ago when I first received her letter was real. This is precisely what moments of knowing do for us.

I believe that KNOWING our impact, our POWER, changes everything. It brings us clarity and peace, because we no longer question ourselves.

While this book ends here, the fears to fierce journey does not. This isn't a process that has a full stop to it; it is cyclical. The 'knowing' moments I have talked about in this chapter, where we no longer question our impact, also provide us with fresh inspiration and invite us to go on another tour of fears to fierce. Each time, we grow from within, and the ripples of our impact spread further than we could ever imagine.

On your fears to fierce journey, you'll have knowing moments of pure understanding, insight and magic, where it'll feel like your fierce is on fire. Look for those glimpses and recognise them as signs of our human interconnectedness.

When we are inspired and we lead ourselves, we inspire others to do the same. That is the greatest impact we can ever have. That is why we choose fierce.

Actions

Commit

Ultimately, it all comes down to you and what you choose to do. That is why each chapter has a list of actions. Not because you have to do them all. In fact, you don't have to do any of them, as long as you do something differently. That could be to decide to start meditating, as I described in chapter 7, or to simply add 'do nothing' on your to-do list. But if you don't change anything, nothing will change.

Remember some of the important lessons we have learned about how we can help ourselves to take action and not procrastinate:

1. **Break it down**: don't get overwhelmed at the size of your vision, take one mini step at a time. Remember Lauri and the cookbook.

2. **Set intentions**: how do you want to feel, and how do you want others to feel?

3. **Visualise the outcome**: the clearer it is in your mind, the easier it will be for you to take action.

4. **Let go of perfection**: it's just another stick we use to beat ourselves with. Aim for good enough instead.

5. **Find someone to hold you accountable:** you'll be far more likely to take action if someone else is expecting something of you. And ask for help when you need it!

6. **Remember your mantra:** fears to fierce.

In addition, never stop trying to become qualified for the job: this is something I read in *Good to Great* by Jim Collins and it made so much sense to me. If we understand ourselves to be life-long learners, making mistakes will be part of what we expect. If we acknowledge 'errors' as inevitable parts of growth, we won't worry so much about them and they won't keep us from taking the first step towards change.

To make it easier to remember the fears to fierce journey, I have designed this diagram to help you visualise it as you practise. This isn't about mastering the first step before you can move on to the next because, as we know, life is messy. Transformation is about change, and so, as you change, so will your power and impact, bringing you closer to your fierce. The fears to fierce journey is not linear or static. This diagram illustrates the broad steps covered in the fears to fierce journey.

The Fears to Fierce Journey

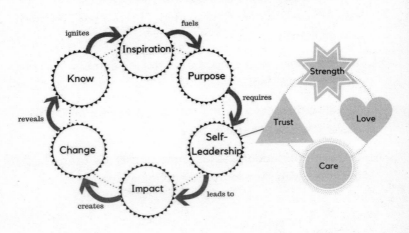

The action tool below is designed to support you on your journey of transformation. Ultimately, the seismic shifts I've outlined in this book come down to you: your commitment, your intentions, your presence, your perseverance. I believe most, if not all, things in life require hard work and commitment. All the inspiration in the world is not going to create change unless you commit to it and take action.

This tool is structured around the chapters in this book. It summarises what you've learned in each chapter, provides you with a condensed version of the actions, prompts you to make commitments/set intentions and write down the actions you've taken, and what happened when you did them. You can take your time and come back to it whenever you wish. It is designed to put into practice the key lessons in each chapter and allow you to personalise it, so it meets your unique needs. Remember, you are in charge!

Your Fears to Fierce Journey

Chapter 1: INSPIRATION

Ignite Your Fierce

Suggested Actions

Goose Bumps
Think about the last time you got goose bumps and write it down. Do this regularly, and you will start to see patterns about what inspires you.

Act on Inspiration
Share with someone else something that inspired you. Note how they respond and how you feel. Reflect on your experience of sharing your inspiration with others – how did they react? How did you feel?

Feed Your Fierce

Social media: Deliberately curate your Instagram and other social media feeds so that you only follow people who inspire you. Unfollow anyone who makes you feel the opposite.

Podcasts: Regularly listen to podcasts that inspire you.

Notebook: When you read something or hear something that inspires you, write it in your notebook. When you are in need of inspiration, take your notebook and randomly open it. Read what you wrote on that page. It will always be exactly what you need to hear in that moment.

Boardroom in your heart: Create a boardroom in your heart with your most important humans who have inspired you deeply. Add humans who will remind you of the different steps on the fears to fierce journey to help you.

Intentions / Commitments

What do you commit to? What are your intentions?

> *For example: I will tell my friend Mary about the inspiring lecture I went to yesterday. I will do this tomorrow in the evening; I will give myself an hour and write down how it felt.*

Report Back

Have you done what you said you would? How do you feel now? What did you learn?

Chapter 2: PURPOSE

Express Your Fierce

Suggested Actions

Define Your Purpose
Sit down and answer the following questions in writing:

- What events have had a key impact on your life?
- Reflect on what you have learned about yourself from these key events. Why do you remember that moment? What do you feel when you think back to it? Write down the feelings – single words are fine. Who are you as a result? What did you learn from that experience? What are the values that you have formed as a result?
- Have a look at the list of words that you have written. Organise them into two lists so that on one side you have the words that describe the experience, and on the other you have the words that describe who you are as a result.
- Circle the words that resonate the most with you
- Write your own purpose statement using those words.

Practise Your Purpose

- Share your purpose statement with someone else. Reflect on how you feel having shared your purpose.
- Pin it up somewhere you'll see it regularly.
- Revisit it as and when you want.
- Make thinking about your purpose a habit.
- Make speaking about your purpose a habit.
- Be inspired by other purposeful self-leaders.
- Add a purposeful leader to the boardroom in your heart.

Intentions / Commitments

What do you commit to? What are your intentions?

> *For example: I will take next Sunday and go through the exercise for formulating my purpose. In a week's time, when I meet with my brother, I will show him my purpose statement.*
>
> *For example: My intention is that even when I feel silly sharing my purpose statement I will do it anyway, because I know I am building a muscle.*

Report Back

Have you done what you said you would? How do you feel now? What did you learn?

Chapter 3: POWER

You Are the Hero of Your Story

Suggested Actions

ALLOW any feelings that come up when you think about your own self-leadership. If you can, write them down.

ACCEPT that change takes time. Be patient with yourself.

ACKNOWLEDGE your progress, your learning, your 'aha' moments. Use your notebook to write them down and regularly reflect on your learning.

ASK for help if the process of 'in-powerment' is hard. You don't have to endure in silence or solitude.

Intentions / Commitments

What do you commit to? What are your intentions?

> *For example: I commit to being kind to myself. I commit to regularly talking to my friend about what I am learning.*

Report Back

Have you done what you said you would? How do you feel now? What did you learn?

Chapter 4: TRUST

You Are Enough, So Trust Yourself Unconditionally

Suggested Actions

Redefine Your Value System

What questions do you hold in your mind, about yourself, that you are waiting for someone else to answer?

Question those questions: write them down. Use the beliefs work to answer your questions:

Beliefs Work

Questions: This is an exercise that will take time. Do not rush it. Use your reflection notebook. You could choose to look at one set of beliefs a day. Write one of the questions at the top of your page and start writing whatever comes to mind. You can start with the questions you identified above and then move on to these:

- What do I believe I need to do/be to be liked?
- What do I believe about myself?
- What do I believe about my health?
- What do I believe about my body?
- What do I believe about myself in my role as a mother/daughter/wife/sister/friend?
- What do I believe about pride, shame, guilt and fear?
- Find other questions that come up as you do this work.

New beliefs: You will discover beliefs that you realise don't serve you. Write that down. I don't want to believe this any longer. Then write down what you want to believe instead going forward.

Practice: You will need to commit to these new beliefs and practise them. You could write them on a piece of paper and hang them up in a place where you see them regularly. Or you could record a voice memo to yourself that you could listen to every morning to help you re-programme your beliefs system.

Tell someone else about this change. Ask them to remind you of this commitment you have made to yourself. Or you can write a letter to yourself with these commitments.

Rewrite your story: Sit down and write a story about yourself. Write about who you are

Mantra: Accept. Breathe. Let go. Trust your fierce. Know you are enough!

Reclaim Your Agency

Listen to the voice in your head: Ask yourself whether you would say these things to your best friend or a person you love. If you would not, make a commitment to practise self-compassion.

Make friends with your ego: Understand your triggers. When you feel triggered, try taking a deep breath and think about where these feelings are coming from. Practise creating a distance between your emotions and your actions.

Understand your attachments: What roles are you attached to? Why are you attached to them? Can you let go of the attachment and trust that you are enough just as YOU?

What would help you to let go of your attachment and do things differently?

Speak out: The next time someone says or does something to you that doesn't sit right, commit to speaking out.

Share your values: Proactively tell those around you about your values and how you like to act in line with them.

Make decisions from a place of trust: Try to practise making decisions from a place of deep trust within yourself.

Intentions / Commitments

What do you commit to? What are your intentions?

For example: I commit to writing about one set of beliefs every evening for the next week.

Report Back

Have you done what you said you would? How do you feel now? What did you learn?

Chapter 5: STRENGTH

You Are Stronger Than You Think

Suggested Actions

Reflect: Think or write about the following questions.

- What fears make you think you are not strong enough? Fear of failure? Or of not being in control? Maybe reading the chapter made you think about your relationship with alcohol?
- Can you see that at the root of it is the fear that you will not be strong enough?

Remember: The next step is to remember one or several times where you have overcome a difficult moment. Try to remember it in as much detail as you can. How it evolved, how you felt, how painful it was, how hard, and the fact that you DID emerge out of it. How do you feel now, looking back on it? Can you see that you were stronger than you thought? Can you capture that feeling for yourself, so you can keep it with you, as a reminder?

Redefine: Maybe the example you just thought of could also help you realise how you might experience that situation differently going forward. Can you find a way to look back on difficult moments as an opportunity to learn and grow rather than as episodes that you are ashamed or embarrassed about?

Stop numbing the pain: Choose one pattern or habit you know you are using to numb your pain. Sit down and think through how you could develop a plan to help yourself let go of the pain suppresser. Revisit the steps I took to stop drinking alcohol. What will you do?

Know your 20-60-20: Identify your growth champions – who are the 20 per cent who believe in you, support you, cheer you on? Who are the 60 per cent who are undecided? And, finally, who are the 20 per cent you know are not on board with you?

Your VIP humans: You can also use Brené Brown's box, where you write down your top VIP humans who you love and respect deeply, whose opinions matter. Keeping this box in your mind, practise going into situations without the fear of not being liked.

Trust your loved ones to be strong: Think about the people you love. What do you do out of the fear that they may not be strong enough? How could you shift that to signal, through your actions and words, that you believe in their strength? Practise this at the next opportunity. When you feel fear rising for a person you love, take a deep breath, let it go and just be present with them.

Practise feeling pain: This is a little bit like detective work. When you feel a niggle, something that doesn't feel right, go there with your attention. Find out where it is coming from. Keep writing and reflecting until you understand your pain.

Intentions / Commitments

What do you commit to? What are your intentions?

For example: I will take time tomorrow evening and do the 20-60-20 exercise to help me understand how best to address the challenges I am currently experiencing at work due to different personalities.

Report Back

Have you done what you said you would? How do you feel now? What did you learn?

Chapter 6: LOVE

Choose Love Every Day

Suggested Actions

Make a gratitude list: Before you fall asleep think of three things that you are grateful for that have happened that day. You can also write them down.

Spread love through appreciation:

- Take a moment – right now – to *send a message* to someone you appreciate. Tell them you're thinking of them and that you love them.
- Try an *'appreciation round'* with your family, friends, or at work. Start by telling the person next to you what you appreciate about them, and they then appreciate the person sitting next to them, and so on until it comes full circle.
- Find other ways to appreciate people around you. For ideas revisit chapter 6.

Practise loving thoughts: Think of someone and feel the love you have for that person, but don't tell them about it. Try doing it in a situation you normally wouldn't – it might feel weird at first but your interaction will be filled with a kindness that wasn't there before.

Release with love: Think about what feelings of anger, resentment, hate you feel attached to. Why do you think you are so attached to them? Who are they directed at? Could you write a letter to that person where you release them with love for yourself and them, just like I did with my mother?

Meet people with love: Consciously practise meeting people with love. When you meet a close family member, focus on love. Then extend the practice to everyone you encounter.

Shower yourself with love: Apply the way you practised sending loving thoughts, warmth and compassion to others to yourself. Close your eyes and imagine warm sunlight enveloping your body, feel the warmth on your skin and inside your body. Feel the love you have so easily for others in your heart and direct it towards yourself. Send yourself loving thoughts.

Help each other to find a way back to love: Who can you ask to help you in moments where you need someone to remind you of your commitment to choosing love? Now go and ask this person to be there for you to remind you.

Intentions / Commitments

What do you commit to? What are your intentions?

> *For example: Tonight I will think of three things I am grateful for before I go to bed.*

Report Back

Have you done what you said you would? How do you feel now? What did you learn?

Chapter 7: CARE

Be Your Own Life Vest

Suggested Actions

Identify your needs: What do you need for yourself to feel better in your body, mind and heart? What brings joy to your fierce?

Be kind to yourself: Remember that sometimes the greatest care is not being harsh on yourself. Never use your care commitments as a stick to beat yourself with.

Deep breaths: Try taking three deep breaths, three times per day.

Try meditation: You can start with five minutes per day. Or just sit for a few minutes every day, noticing your breath and how your body feels. Try downloading an app that can accompany you.

Reflections: Use your notebook and pen to write down your thoughts and feelings. Keep writing until it feels 'sticky'.

Do something new: What is the thing you have always wanted to do? Start the process of getting you to the place where you will do it: book it, pay the deposit or tell a person who will hold you accountable. But do it now. Then message me on Instagram @britafs and tell me about it!

Find your exercise: Give yourself time to find out what exercise routine works for you.

Watch your energy: Think back to a time where you met up with someone and afterwards came home feeling exhausted. Ask yourself why that is. Next time you meet that person, remember how he or she makes you feel. Ask yourself what you can do to minimise their impact on you.

Be accountable: Find someone who you are going to be accountable to for your care commitments. Report to them daily, or as often as you can.

Intentions / Commitments

What do you commit to? What are your intentions?

For example: I will book the thing I have always wanted to do right now and I will tell my friend that I am going to do it and ask her to remind me if I am tempted to cancel it later.

Report Back

Have you done what you said you would? How do you feel now? What did you learn?

Chapter 8: IMPACT

You Matter

Suggested Actions

Practise Self-Awareness

- Think back to a recent meeting you had. When you arrived, what did you say, do, think, and how did the person respond? What sense did you get from them? How do you think you made that person feel? What did they do?
- Think about a meeting that you have coming up – commit to being aware and observe your impact on that person. If you can, write it down.
- Think about people who have given you feedback. What do they tell you about yourself? Does that resonate? If it doesn't, where is the dissonance? Can you reconcile it? Ask yourself why you think that people perceive you in this way?

Practise Setting Intentions
Identify an event/conversation/meeting that you want to set an intention for. Ask yourself:

How do I want to be in that moment? How do I want the other(s) to feel as a result of my behaviour there? What do I want the outcome(s) to be for that moment?

Set the intention to make space for self-awareness during the event and be detached from the outcome.

Visualise your intentions: Close your eyes and see yourself in that moment. Feel how you will feel if you realise your intentions. The clearer your visualisation, the easier it will be to call it up during that moment; writing it down or drawing something is also helpful.

Growing Your Fierce Impact
Your beliefs: What do you believe about power and its impact, and about YOUR power and its impact?

Your leadership alchemy: Looking back over the notes you've been making as you've worked through the action plan in each chapter, write down some words that you think represent your 'leadership alchemy'.

Try it out and make a habit of it: Identify the earliest opportunity to put your impact to the test. Do you have an event, or a meeting, a task or a call coming up where you can practise your leadership alchemy intentionally? Decide now when you will do this. Set the date. Commit. As soon as you have done it once, make a habit of it.

Embrace challenges: Note when people feel challenged by your impact. Why do you think they feel challenged? What is it telling you about your impact, and about them? Try the 'Hold' exercise when you next feel your power is under threat.

Visualise your protective armour: When you notice that challenging responses are getting you down, use this visualisation technique. Close your eyes and imagine you are wearing a protective armour; this can be whatever you want it to be.

Intentions / Commitments

What do you commit to? What are your intentions?

> *For example: At the next meeting with Rosie, I will be aware of my impact and protect myself. I will practise the 'Hold' exercise.*

Report Back

Have you done what you said you would? How do you feel now? What did you learn?

Chapter 9: CHANGE

Together We Embrace Our Shared Humanity

Suggested Actions

Act: The next time you feel empathy rising within you, act on it. Some scenarios might include:

- Saying hello to a homeless person you pass in the street. Or simply looking them in the eye and acknowledging them. Create a connection with someone you normally would not.
- When you see a colleague struggling, and your instinct is to offer to help her or him, do it. Go up to her or him and ask if you can help them.
- When you notice someone has been in the toilet for a long time and you think there is something wrong with them, follow your sense and ask them.

Think about what you *didn't* do: Was there a recent occasion where you had the instinct to take action and then didn't? Go back to it now and do it. Acting on your instinct to help is a muscle you need to build up. The more you do it, the better.

Come up with your own ideas: Think about something that is important to you and you would like to change. This could be about the environment in which you live, or it could be about something further removed from you. Research how you might take action. Then take the first step.

Nurture that feeling of sisterhood: Learn to understand how you feel when you see your fierce reflected in someone else. Who comes to your mind when you think about that deep connection? Have you seen them recently? Make time to see them because they are your cheerleaders and just being in their presence will help you on your journey.

Make a list of causes you feel a connection with, writing down why and what you would like to do for them. Identify your top one and get in touch with the people running it to find out how you might get involved.

Don't take no for an answer: Whether it's the voice in your head, or the voice on the other end of the phone, do not take no for an answer.

Intentions / Commitments

What do you commit to? What are your intentions?

For example: By the end of the week I will have responded to that letter asking me to donate.

Report Back

Have you done what you said you would? How do you feel now? What did you learn?

Chapter 10: KNOW

You Are Fierce

Suggested Actions

Be present – and you'll notice these moments of knowing as they arise. Think of them as signs that confirm you're on the right path.

This is about reaping the rewards of all your work, commitment, reflections and action!

Intentions / Commitments

What do you commit to? What are your intentions?

Report Back

Have you done what you said you would? How do you feel now? What did you learn?

My sources of inspiration

Here I share with you some of my favourite sources of inspiration which in one way or another have changed my life. I hope they will inspire you too.

Books

Mitch Albom, *Tuesdays with Morrie* (Sphere, 2003)

Gillian Anderson and Jennifer Nadel, *We: A Manifesto for Women Everywhere* (Harper Thorsons, 2017)

Mark Anthony, *The Beautiful Truth* (Create Space, 2016)

Mary Beard, *Women & Power: A Manifesto* (Profile Books, 2018)

Gabrielle Bernstein, *The Universe Has Your Back* (Hay House, 2016)

Jill Bolte Taylor, *My Stroke of Insight* (Hodder Paperbacks, 2009)

Brené Brown, *Rising Strong* (Vermilion, 2015); *Braving the Wilderness* (Vermilion, 2017)

Rebecca Campbell, *Rise Sister Rise* (Hay House, 2016)

Christine Carter, *The Sweet Spot* (Ballantine Books, 2017)

Soraya Chemaly, *Rage Becomes Her* (Simon & Schuster, 2018)

Pema Chodron, *The Places that Scare You* (HarperNonFiction, 2004)

Jim Collins, *Good to Great* (Random House Business, 2001)

Sam Collins, *Radio Heaven* (Motivational Press, Inc., 2015)

Stephen Covey, *The 7 Habits of Highly Effective People* (Simon & Schuster, 2004)

Glennon Doyle, *Love Warrior* (Two Roads, 2017) and *Untamed* (Vermilion, 2020)

Edith Eger, *The Choice* (Rider, 2017)

Viktor Frankl, *Man's Search for Meaning* (Rider, 2004)

Demetra George, *Mysteries of the Dark Moon* (Bravo Ltd, 1992)

Elizabeth Gilbert, *Big Magic* (Bloomsbury Paperbacks, 2016)

Daniel Goleman, *Emotional Intelligence* (Bloomsbury Publishing, 1996)

Jayne Hardy, *The Self-Care Project* (Orion Spring 2017)

Jeremy Heimans & Henry Timms, *New Power*, (Macmillan 2018)

Jean Houston, *The Wizard of Us* (Atria Books, 2016)

Susan Jeffers, *Feel the Fear and Do It Anyway* (Hutchinson, 1987)

Rupi Kaur, *Milk and Honey* (Andrews McMeel Publishing, 2015) and *The Sun and Her Flowers* (Simon & Schuster, 2017)

Nancy Kline, *Time to Think* (Cassell, 2002)

Catherine Mayer, *Attack of the 50ft Women* (HQ, 2018)

Kristin Neff, *Self Compassion* (Yellow Kite, 2011)

Thich Nhat Hanh, *Reconciliation* (Parallax Press, 2010)

Michelle Obama, *Becoming* (Viking, 2018)

Alex Soojung-Kim Pang, *Rest* (Penguin Life, 2018)

Grayson Perry, *The Descent of Man* (Penguin, 2017)

Philippa Perry, *The Book You Wish Your Parents Had Read* (Penguin Life, 2019)

Robert E. Quinn, *Deep Change* (John Wiley & Sons, 1996)

Don Miguel Ruiz, *The Four Agreements* (Amber-Allen Publishing, Inc., 2018)

Zainab Salbi, *Between Two Worlds: Escape from Tyranny – Growing Up in the Shadow of Saddam* (Avery, 2006)

June Sarpong, *The Power of Women* (HQ, 2018)

Rebecca Solnit, *The Mother of All Questions*, (Granta Books, 2017) and *Hope in the Dark* (Canongate Books, 2016)

Melis Senova, *This Human* (BIS Publishers, 2017)

Chade-Meng Tan, *Search Inside Yourself* (HarperOne, 2014)

Eckhart Tolle, *A New Earth* (Penguin, 2009)

Shefali Tsabary, *The Conscious Parent* (Yellow Kite, 2015)

Poem:

Ev'Yan Whitney, 'The Too Much Woman' www.simonasiclari.com/the-too-much-woman-evyan-whitney

Podcasts

Oprah Winfrey's *SuperSoul Sundays* podcast (in particular the two episodes with Mark Nepo, and the series with Eckhart Tolle about *A New Earth*)

Ctrl Alt Delete with Emma Gannon

Desert Island Discs

Gurls Talk with Adwoa Aboah

How to Fail with Elizabeth Day

How to Own the Room with Viv Groskop

How I Found My Voice with Intelligence Squared

In Good Company with Otegha Uwagba

Masters of Scale with Reid Hoffman

Sisterhood Works with The Albright

The Guilty Feminist with Deborah Frances-White

The Happy Podcast with Fearne Cotton

Unlocking Us with Brené Brown

Under the Skin with Russell Brand

Work Like a Woman with Mary Portas

Mentors/Coaches:

Dr Sam Colins www.drsamcollins.com

Gosia Gorna www.gosiagorna.com

Melis Senova www.melissenova.com

Moira Spence www.moiraspence.com

Katy Meade-King www.soulspirit.co.uk

My gratitude list

Yay! I get to do my own gratitude list. As you know, gratitude is practising love, and there is an awful lot of love that I feel for all the incredible, wonderful humans who have cheered me on, supported me, nurtured me, gently guided me and lovingly critiqued me. First up is:

The dream team

I feel so deeply grateful for the core team, who guided me through the maze that was writing my first book. I met Valeria Huerta, my wonderful agent, for the first time in early 2017 and it was love at first sight. Her immediate endorsement of me and my idea gave me the courage to believe that perhaps I could write a book. Cyan Turan, my genius editor, thank you for making everything more beautiful, smooth and simple. Olivia Morris, my brilliant publisher, thank you for your belief in me, for championing my book and for your wise counsel. I thought writing a book would be lonely, I was wrong. You three are my fierce dream team.

Thank you also to everyone at Rider, in particular Anna Bowen, Ellie Crisp, Bianca Bexton and Lorraine Jerram.

The women in my boardroom

My deepest gratitude and love for the incredible women in my boardroom, who have inspired me so deeply and gave me the courage to follow my fierce.

Above all thank you Amela, my sister, for allowing me to share our story. You told me about your happiness that our story of sisterhood and friendship, from two different worlds, will remain to live on after us in this book. I am forever grateful to be connected to you.

My champions, cheerleaders and fierce feminists

I feel so immensely lucky to have around me such an incredible tribe of women and men who are my champions, my cheerleaders, fierce feminists and sisters. You have all helped me in some way on this journey and, without you, I would not have been able to write *Fears to Fierce*. Thank you to my guides and wise women: Dr Sam Collins, Gosia Gorna, Tina Wallace, Moira Spence, Melis Senova and Katy Meade. Thank you to my friends, you gave me so much love and encouragement: Lauri Pastrone, Shivonne Graham, Joey Bose, Paulina Stachnik, Catherine Pearson, Amelia Nice, Gabi Dornheim, Manuela Nissen, Tanya Mackay, Nadimeh Zeytoun, Han Jeong-won, Iliriana Gashi, Seida Saric, Preeti Malkani. Thank you for your wise counsel and insight: Ruth Tyson, Brigid Moss, Izzy Clark, Lynn Tabbara, Jasmine Hemsley, Nick Hopper. Thank you for your inspiration: Zoja, Remzije, Latif, Sarah Clark, Ceri Hayes. Thank you for your support: Negar Sharafi, Maggie Baxter, Martin Thomas. To all the women I have coached: thank you, you have inspired me with your fierce transformation. Thank you to all my colleagues around the world at Women for Women International, you inspire me daily and I am deeply grateful to work as part of such an incredible team. My gratitude also goes to all the women who have read an early proof and have supported me with their love and kindness!

A special thank you to Gillian Anderson and Jennifer Nadel for writing the foreword to my book, which is definitely one of those magic moments, where dreams come true. Thank you.

My family

Anyone who has ever undertaken a big project like writing a book, while also holding down a full-time job and having a family, knows that without real hard-core support from your family, it won't be possible. I am so grateful to my family, who have supported me throughout in so many different ways. Thank you to my brother Alex, my sister-in-law Ann and my nephew Lucas and my niece Lotte for allowing me to stay in their gorgeous house by the sea, where I was able to write in peace for a few weeks. Thank you to my mum for setting the example. Because you wrote a book, I believed that I could do so too. And, above all, thank you to my daughters Emma and Sara and to Jose Luis. It's not just putting up with me sitting at my computer for hours during holidays and weekends over the past three years, it is also adapting to a continuously transforming me, who is learning as I go along, which I know can be unsettling. My deepest gratitude is for that. That you stand by me. Thank you.

About the Author

Driven by her purpose, Brita believes that every woman has a fierce power to fulfil her dreams. She coaches women to help them transform their lives by awakening and acting on the power they have within. Brita is an advocate and promoter of women's power, women's rights and equality. She frequently writes and speaks publicly about the challenges women face all over the world in the context of poverty and conflict.

Originally from Germany, Brita went to school in Venezuela and throughout her career has worked with women from many countries around the world. She now lives in the UK with her husband, two daughters and two dogs.

Brita currently serves as the Executive Director of Women for Women International – UK and is the Senior Vice President for Europe and External Relations globally. She co-founded Women for Women International in Germany in 2018.

Fears to Fierce is her first book, it is personal and the views represented in the book do not necessarily reflect the views of the organisations she works for.

About Women for Women International

When there is an outbreak of war or violence, women suffer most – they experience trauma, sexual violence and the death of loved ones. After the conflict is over, the world's attention moves on, but women are left to rebuild their families and communities.

Women for Women International supports women who live in some of the world's most dangerous places. Women enrol on the charity's year-long training programme, where they learn how to earn and save money, improve their family's health and make their voices heard at home and in their community.

Since 1993, the charity has helped over half a million marginalised women survivors of war in Afghanistan, Bosnia and Herzegovina, the Democratic Republic of Congo, Iraq, Kosovo, Nigeria, Rwanda and South Sudan.

With over fifty brutal armed conflicts across the globe, there's never been a greater need to support women survivors of war. With your help, women can graduate from the Women for Women International programme with the skills, knowledge and resources to become successful entrepreneurs. They will pass on their knowledge to their neighbours and children, creating a ripple effect.

You can help to change the world by sponsoring one woman, your new 'sister' to take part in the Women for Women International programme. Your monthly gift of £22 will help your sister learn skills so she can rebuild her life and inspire hope for the future. She will learn about four key topics; how to protect her health, how to stand up for her rights, how to earn and save money and the power of support networks.

Like Brita and Amela's story, not only will you help to change your sister's life, she will also change yours. You will develop a personal connection that transcends continents by writing messages of support and encouragement to your sister. If she is able, she will write back to you, and share the impact of what she is learning with your support.

Sponsor a woman survivor of war today: www.womenfor-women.org.uk/fears-to-fierce

Find out more at womenforwomen.org.uk or follow @WomenforWomenUK on social media.

UK Charity Registration Number: 1115109